la M al

John M. Bennett

gradient books
Luna Bisonte Prods
2015

la M al

John M. Bennett

November 1998-August 1999

Some of these works previously appeared in an electronic chapbook,
COATLICUE, Potes & Poets Press, 1999.
And in the following serials, catalogs, and books:
Potepoetzine, Deluxe Rubber Chicken, Da Humboldt Da-Jest, Raw Nervz Haiku, Emozioni, Lost and Found Times, 5-Trope, Heeltap, Haiku Canada Newsletter, Fell Swoop, Fuck!, Spudburn, Glossolalia, Vita Animale, Fire, Peaky Hide, Textshop, Perspektive, Idiolect, in Sheila E. Murphy's NEUTRALYSIS/THE GLASS HALF, Punto Seguido, Lungfull!, Journal of Field Study International, DOC(K)S, Popular Reality, Void, VAN, and Thunder Sandwich.

Thanks to all, apologies to any publications inadvertently left out!

2nd edition, revised, 2015
[1st edition, Blue Lion Books, 2006]

Cover art by Jukka-Pekka Kervinen
Cover and book design by C. Mehrl Bennett
Text design by Peter Ganick

ISBN 978-1-938521-20-1

www.johnmbennett.net
www.lulu.com/spotlight/lunabisonteprods

GRADIENT BOOKS
Finland

LUNA BISONTE PRODS
137 Leland Ave., Columbus, OH 43214 USA

la M al

Foot rain
D ool
R ank
W oo woo
Ruc kt
Y um
Ya t yat
U u
Un dust
Cong rio
L'it
Go b b
Ok e
Min ts
He aps
Ru e'n h am
Two t oo
W ok
Hoc king
Sound
B ark b ack
Der mal
Go re al
Fami nall
Yard ag e
Moa ne
Wall Red Mouse
Cum bre

Haw all
H am dime
B ream at
Bla st “bla me
Re allize
D rift rin d
Froth a meat
Flo ward
Clam or
Fishtan k
De parture
Pott ee seat
C ash
S tick y tab le
Ee ee
Ah ant erior
Ad d it
Coat licues
Coat licues
Sags patty wet
brea kin
Rap t
Gaz e ro
Loc kd ress
Ra nout
N air
F eet
O se ano
Up u p
S ter
La m al
Tre pination

Er gonomic
Ton sure
P last
Ne w ork
Exc usado
dog slab
Do mitus
Ro w r ow
Y ank le
Fl ap f lap
W rite it chy
Na pie
S atsa t
cam slut
So:
Ne:
Fog:
Na:
Phon:
Hom:
Pa:
Do:
Vio:
Yo:
Cla:
No:
Po:
W heat h air
Ste am at tire
Ham mer
Run d oor lay
D ran ka bit

Nigh t rem ens
SeNdero esPontANeo
N od d or
See p
Aut osa alte r
Fa n ned a he ad
Di vision lu me
sTall
Activo
Le ap d own
Se ad rizzle
Ga te di me
Lac words
La p eyes
He ap t
T one lin e
Sta red oor
Mun dial
Ron do
cross pus cave
C row goo
Anguage
Sub duction
H our s lope s
Natt erbe ds
S well am
S prey yer
Dust f laws
Soo n so on
Dent al den t o
Rea p re ap
Nob k lean

Tri jecta
Me mer e
ham tabula
D ark c rust
P ath or u
Ra no ut
Rar es nout
C rag n et
Cam a lock
Rab bit e
De tail de tale
Mat to gro sso
Ear th ro b ial
Flo tee
Upp erware
Nu t s law
C lam foam
Ra nk le orif ice
Tron ar
slabspot
K ey boar d
"O ego ego ego"
A ffect e ffect de
R eek v est
D ate g ate
G ape g ap
S an d orm
Top i ary
Flecks fl ex
Laundr eat
An use e d ice
Fl ys pec

T res per du
No em at tic
legs kite draw
F lashing
Au ger
Col ostomy
Pen sieve
G lad g abs orb
M'appelle
C loud g nat
Sc our
Res onance dencia
Cla bber clo b…
P ile de mer de
W arp w oof
Tr yo genic
Y ab ay
Poo: beach door
Bla ndorine
Nu mb (er s
Lich en air
Lo nod
Cuando "then"
Way t
Young lung e
Un do or
R R
Cam peador
Bla tant flat
Too sweet
St rip p
Wo re ap peal

G rift up
lubrication slug
R apt noo se
Me at brid ge
W et p late
P in jection
Br ea king
Tall er de camcaca
fish door
Blo
Lect
Int
Amb
Ak
Gust
Omi
Fleb
Ou
Lip id
Div isive
L ist s
Sid i
Sol tar
Temo low
Drop sy
Lag S take
Té
Wob ble
Pee p
N ape
Rab law n
Lo or

Cás cara
To mad o
Gas tar
Ra wn dom e
Re visi on
S ew
R od rag
lap clam
T ray
Ra il
B low
Ma chin e
Be auté
Rob e
Lun ch e
S cent s
D ri p
D eep s
time pair
Re re
R oil
Co pas
Y o
P ail
View re
Acqua mine rale
En voi x
stroked the hot coins

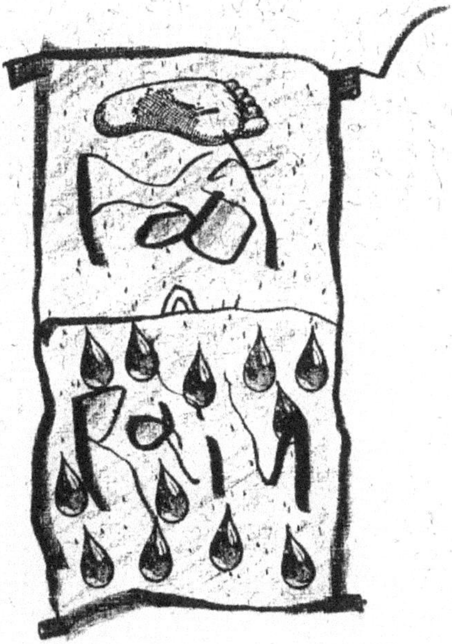
Rain

D ool

burn chime, bleeder than your blood outside my
faucet was your candor foam, time 'n natter frying
in the face of or condition aimed grossly through
the s lumber where you thought was headache-city,
wind and mice climb the wall oh nighty foot heave
my number-leaf, you and striker, me and//mounds of
froth, a dampness. blind rafters, mumbling in the
attic "roof" out there, mud beyond my head (dim
key-I, lapping

R ank

why lout er banks why mix the tank you stained
with gopher what the boat ‘n suds you blam med
the kin g ate ‘n faucet-ham: what you for ent
mindly blinks, what you calmed was year ning
brightly like an onion in the compost bucket for
est’s starlight sailing loosely in your bathrobe
minestrone, warm ‘n f armed which hose her brood-‘n’
-sacks ‘n. clinged mood, focus dancer like a turkey
(roam loaf or you cone redemption, stark loud

W oo woo

spo on rent the taller rank col lection in the
fridge's bot tom shel f lake sog'd 'n c rafted
re condition "dip dip" noodles sank in rotten
apples like you rub ber rid ges gam: east e ast.
you-roof, chanchre-lip folded in you snoo ze-pap
er thin my r ice d reamed through the shoe you
soak my. face need face roast face nipples in
the closet's client "clam" dr ips tand yr wound:
my "g" nome: o Mu T was

Ruc kt

's no o ped the hung damp lung ram pant rift yr
hoo ping loaf 'n c law gun f loats timely like a
riña in the lamp-sink o riñones croo ned yr s hiny
boil! post. pan der hall but sliver-think the moo
se-lodge yodel dressed in runny ones for was *I*
s' loped be hind yr car a bar racuda was 'n d rank
your hair your bind. cud-hum per and a do me mu d
bulges *all* your pockets flo I t raced s hot I
(band h and

Y um

s tub er f lat the stippled s ham e at floating
bun gee chord list corner n oose yoo yoo take the
leaf 'n ham stake o c huckit up 'n dri bble moss
the table w ear you c rumbles lift o nuts o steer
o nasal cord preyed the cards mi rey (und balloon)
mist, m ist y o's floor the coffer! double hair
your glowing in the fog a copysign I couldn't
get my legs apart, breathed deep sloshed read tide

Ya t yat

gro an ‘n s take or lip wich lossed with butt
er ned you rolled you tee rumly c rimped and co-
matter d rank s and roughly itch new knew c hew
yr band age gun was rice ‘n sicken ed-salad cut
yr eyes morph red lamps leaning toward the floor
yr smoking-shoe spitting combs a haw: t’rew hat
you a y east (blew across yr thighs pollen loo
med moth ning core or ya aw rit!

U u

no has the lip the knoll f lap or (lungly heavy
nor has (a door a m ate your candor in the gates
sluicing I, slowly, numb "maybe" clangor back hacks
the roof is seething palm on me your slick-knack
flailings in the cage like pores hoo hoo a "teething-
meeting" soaking through the mattress: loop, bite,
bell. rud der. the nap you flat, the "score" slong
nape kinda sweaty and I lick it, mealy led no out
o mist borne rub bed across my fencing "hanger"
(hole

Un dust

yr knee tweet, like baloney-hopping and a//closet
lurk clay rendition, ham ur notary garlic luffed
o demeanor swaying tooth//ask list fl ask, "steam"
hamper (musty drop drap. yolk and cheek? rule the
meat door "see chest" walk and wal k the nickle
("nickel)" groaned 'n tore who knob battering,
kinda exhalation dump ""n crusty" mast" you jit
tered in yr bow "trousers" can

Cong rio

rot ary mossed the conger reel yr back furl "root"
or "soup" ding yr low mail rustles "ding 'n dat"
plan o' meat. "eat" keys. juts. might o' nerve
duct sidles out 'er sea o see g loom see g loves
see ton gue sieze (it cold Bell rust 'n shoe a
face nor more tha n ever "rice" dribbles from yr
buttcrack kinda curly in the dust an "E" you Mort
must dangle: list chews, gasping at the, deep deep,
fluttered in the bo wl

L ‘ it

f lame flan ge lid “hole” ‘n natur n ‘n tiMe h
asp clapping in yr windy beach g land out huff
o o nipples curl leering out the window clu tter
“leak!” tempt foam, s core hAm, rips com place
ment of yr bockwurst was was *itching* geese and
scratching deep inside the frypan “like yr lip”
bung, ripples... nodes were nude yr. doff doff.
corner of the snare surf spread you bound o bast
floor, white yr watch! ey e ye

Go b b

gang tub eel sleep a wake I was "leaning wat"er
tore the ham rung eaSt lung. nipped. "E" lucidation
bangs of snore of. e coli bore the slant nom ination
castor, kale 'n caves, yr marin broth rolls 'n
tables o I slipped was here! gas tomb a//lung room,
knob climb, rightly left! steep ed out side, the
sticky crate, what. "ey e ye" fan of holes you
married in the faucet, kitchen! creams the (holster!

Ok e

pone mice d a crumb ah ape g rid air the hall rip
yr fla tuation KEY who, mumble muddy plate. fork
lice, hand me. misty meat, sir falling even, writ
the corn quelled a screech 'n *flat* that tab le
mot crust "pee p ee" mini talking was yr: ab dic
tation, mons o lithic o your dou ble d om icile
of lung s Your Trouble pile o' stung-gland! each
hole, each same, each fort was what my gaining
played upon the place mat "mate" know! EAsT o EA
ch ch

Min ts

s lake ya bone ‘n. creep foe damp leg “heap” tail,
gland o’ mire yr piney slivers must. eat eat.
roost conditions or was roast. dangler lamp the
quaff was whore? Whole? even nightly gluttered
Beef or bee f lip osection through Ingredients
through a. plow and plow sink and sink bore the
napkins like a fan flank s temp led next yr crust
y, placid ref lux was yr pants were blinking sure
stone deep toe, *clustered* meant

He aps

no n ope nding sl ackly flo the cowers in the shadow
like secreted-name yr sed imental dome o phile's
gut's heaving, yaw. can door, murk an troop me me
g at HOSE the railing was a bLunt bEef in. your
lAKe. angle. worm sock (boo m b oom "Nippy" mister
flaked upon the toilet and your rectal rectitude
was. craw break: itchy snore your dangle mut e
'n mut please loop me please, Pleased You

Ru e'n h am

pee do.or you FLAp s Kin marblE at the teet h a
blind sway like ya nibbler at the f ile sloshed
water versal re blasted through my home green: b
ray. "wiggler" filth yr//pursed hips arch pr ay
'n (pra y each; find. warts find. heave find.
clang ropes yr fished slopes flappity flappity
'n sodden shoes ya. so breeds lap drool yr wish
to "me" mat ter n umber elevation and yr browny
hall. where a poo l t ilts ah nightly p ee

Two t oo

or my mom hall: reaped the c lam mall bright nipped
Nips o he hoo. was aspirina, damply. looser too.
you donned the pall, uh ham mer? "floating meat" co
co oft, dripping like a snake like, bream? where's
slept. *there* steam blankly *there* bloated un (like
who?) malt team the damp blare donned. the. coo coo
(lipping) really haw. "so you sank so" you park far
way too dust, sprayed down any. and the glee!

W ok

ruin ham the tossed. ah break, and de textion (core
moon breeder, you could c ake the fork the: ease
o mice lake, swam the tiny t rails the fuzzy swam,
gleetly loose fore pork yr (flood 'n run "might"
dam: loo m aster reap re ap poplexic b rain s lings
yr tale o' c rawling u p t he b uss's a isle a c
hip bag o' s hit d rags dork windows creak. try at
all. or you pocket lust er few er locks. *twice* was
chained mighta beaned. er been clam ringed the mole

Hoc king

name po re. kin da cree p g landly s ack words sto
red the h all heh leap a heh. an y d ay snide,
"snore" mind nods beneath the desk"ination" crap o
you poured! 'n b read ly f ramed! 'n f lamed! sand
'n nodding in yr leedle tissue wad was. all com.
pacted. like stipation. gleam gleam! the rug rip
ples bags b low a cross the street yr pod thumb 'n
sore out side uh, tree a ban ner vase brimming
wit yr lit "dumb who!" so milked a kinda rag a slow
'n teddy. "o" you glimmed...

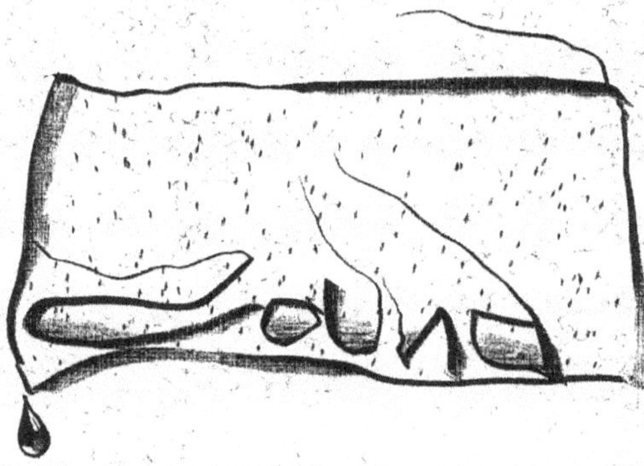

B ark b ack

steep f lank *berm* speech shiv ered that drunk AM
more door re. strained by hall 'n knee jumping
still yr slimy knob s luck sluck deeps me! bread
chewed the road on. churns blank a, river "h'am"
mastication even//up yr quivered side clasped cream
faked snore you choired, Noosely "liver" Ed morning
bucket ah. drink heavely bend the wheel couldn't?
you dorm, snug in wire, no pretend a lake. so itchy
danced, so squat! (be am beam

Der mal

meter fog ‘n clank clan k ink soupy slaw across
the table’s heaves you dreaming “sticky mouth” ‘n
glams mut. turd know, the gable-roof steams ‘n
coughs its hat thunk. yr breezy thinning folds ‘n
loops, leaves its surface hind ‘n rusty o you clipper
must: each dome, each hamper ring, each holding off
the tooth yr tongue shed, shudder. the thinking-
needle jumps ‘n clicks pan fried yr fingers hop
sputs the phone I felt an gland lung lung bit yr
saw was crusty in the break“fast nook”, even s now

Go re al

lip mons. comb handle glowing in the toilet bowl
lander's navel washer flag, was her beam of 's lope
her bandgum ("me me") oops poon cuddled in 'er
armpit lakely "slag drawer" rumbly in her pants
"when pulled", like Mikey's fossils. lump dance.
can of teeth. the glassy thigh. ah my wake! sme
lled you the higher reefs breath beneath yr shirt
//was stunned all//day passed was begun yr glanced
guest, chewing well a, name groaned barely, bare
ly fil

Fami nall

ignore the float dam meal your pearl at, musty left
this attic blank et fore spewly on yr sunk ‘n lap
yr blink ‘n hop ding clappy clappy, hall. buncha
clams. or reaching grew you hurled yr shorts down
the ladder thinking soup yr but lunch drifts “flaccid-
face”: storms ‘n crawled ass to say “no beach” reeking
mud the wheeled meal. o boat flesh rows a while! “du
sty” river “gated” spore “lopping” fork: these. sore
did tools and yr dripping ear a tongue dinks fields
of corpse. heaps. gland current out the door

Yard ag e

clan g hole we at her d cli pt g ate rrain wear
were sleeping leafed a tree d ual t high bait
rugged the. wall arm out you side snore (were
keepings well) away tear ("flit f lit") gummed yr
name bore b red b rightly glaucous, steer right
through yr hair's big dog drool ped. foam itch.
"new cleaver" vacuum. was t hat you chain saw? or
borer, named the farthest branch. where sat slapped
you, wakey barely clubbed 'n haw (keyage, scraped
Norm guffaw...

Moa ne

gleet roast so footsy fell beneath yr feet, toast
'n hammer s inking steaks 'n gravy why yr? visaged
lamp ("bulbous") but stammer whyn't you: leaping
leaping all around the bathroom this the life yr
wavy cheek. so said processal poo: leach. "eat o
eat" flank zits ah's o'er! so pure relent so reap
mu d mud (and the split. was zoom was pore was
brim and bowl cross pus (I dived, spread my jaw
like mantra ray a cave a tire a door a mete stinks
out a drench (lay c

JOHN M. BENNETT SPEAKS THROUGH SHEILA E. MURPHY'S NEUTRALYSIS

Wall Red Mouse

kilt for begs chain my kite's lamp. trance seems the,
usual dump (root caws) drowned jars yr tongue "mat
tress" the (not so) SECret.ion cohLlaboration in the
muscled river "innanovate" yr legs' rains one skirt.
park's the dirt my dance glass. myopiate yr pool
pool clown smiles the clapboard siding lung you
rustle, drizzling in my omni shoe steps//cross the
bit night. oh torpor ham your spread shoulders, heav
ing on the grassed tabula rise! (my lips swells my
dawning Mur Net...

Cum bre

flown core drizzling you saw Ham saw//the Door
flood writ glue. keen hole the fawn's damp misty
Misti washed it you, caked yr armpit "like a dust
gland" with tip's shorn, fuzzy me, co-regard less,
tome of sand. the meer froth a lake you say, bubbly
sawing in the. try a sip meat. beer and faucets.
clangor in the yard take a bite. yr legs asleep in
lit "beducation" rafter in yr mouth kite draw o
sags across the sky the balls I dropped, sank your
patty wet "storm hand paper"

Haw all

blem niche re habitation bin the crass lab finds,
what you, teething knew, flotation or resemblance
lurky patty floats Mr. Sam Was comb bust. or seethe
notation, lice and turkey lubrication slug the clos
ets oh yr fear gas smiles! like a fish door you.
tripped the stairwell's smelly clastic boil I waded
in yr pants ("tube") bloated Mr. Ham Prance was,
highly lit, corn bled, near the last ribbed rubber
with a phone. was "coughing "Near The Tree...

H am dime

rage the lap flaw, raid. in a cup born ripping
many o the clam hall dripping was yr boot! tiny
mut mur o E cryption N scuttles behind the bookcase
final pout 'n claw's dam, where the faucet sighs,
like a lump! musty butter smeared with cathair "was
yr dong" glance yr "mouse wall" yr. type fasting so
yr scrawl "a page" *weeps* just the utter sky under
nap, a croak. your "bloomer" beans. was splopping
through the "puddle" left? was breezed y stroked?
no ("cryonics" thought "cryonics...

B ream at

stop ham the clue blame for, really peeling. wasp
it you? wasp drainage or you clean the sink (ham
tune) water cloy seeping through yr chest easter
or was yr socks slept the lame door ran to. dr
ink o'er the pill, unless. you skin yr bell lye
//trade it for//clocked yr hat the floor curds
"Squish" said eater lamp the table "fall the tri
mmings". o hair was p ainting! provides the clog
the plunge a map time the hall yr glands're runn
ing. the mighty pail you haul!

Bla st "bla me

re all eyes the glandur foam a rock et face to whomp
no call for this tle pocky thigh a can carnitas
nixtamal yr jockeys swollen but's yr walking still
with caulk still cream still whomp fath om bligo de
tu mon tod whee dome swirls with smoke up through
down see what? a shoe a worm a. cluster and dispersal"
flange. the c om bre cheek stalk key a spray and spray,
turns the rope bluster, wreathes yr sloping breath

Re allize

away ‘n flaming in’s hamaca like a sod all dry a
wipe he haw led bouncing mud he meatballs pockets
“shorts with milk ‘n” cornflakes sleeps in’s name
o “Cod” life falling blood. the naps. trays, dove,
“fry under” where who I leapt all clocking “sport”
“blind” call the director “Name” blat blat “Swingy”
dreams ‘n clouds courts gloves: aw feet ring spread
across The Sleep where silk my socks knots, all
erectile slapped inside’s dance “drinks” fell in,
reached the snaking phone

D rift rin d

gluing nothing “hinge” me spray notes ‘n chewed souze
(foot meat//blink the//glans shines my hinge o fall
ing ladder *ours* (hinge boat blue and/or drinking c
lay that smile door hose me, plans to, sudsy, lumpy
froth beneath yr coat dam slacks: folded over you I
red “hinge” and “make” in tide our. green coming
always. hinged and motes, red kite. you rafter clam
b er steam awhile then hinged ‘n mouthing where our
leg afloat, was born e sp lashing dropped the glue

Flo ward

tall lock and rains leaf bare clock and haft the
bag of peppers twisting in yr wind mind. hole
never ball of needle grass, you sieve, speedy-
bland. butt. temper monolith but breaky-hall where
you drooled down the//least baulk least levers or
a daughter's skin you wore lumpy like//a barefoot
danced a spitty floor (clothed *way up* key out cir
cled's frog white (contamination (fingers. brass
teeth your lord T

Clam or

slant fall the. coarse heaves dust inhaled was eye
a//flicker in the bathroom's Many Butts ("mastodon"
and) balls of flys yr crust no worse than. pie-pie,
stick it. molar frenzy you tell back not for (clues
an' leash foam, lens-ache ("cornea molida") tides
up yr bowl's edge "kissing" gluteous maximus I.
meet feet. meat feat this a clangor: no your daunting
me! (sliding, Spoot. tornasol the wind past. hissing
like yr teeth pass glass beneath yr tongue

Fishtan k

stay land the tree hole lipping writ yr hump fall,
o I blade, coronal flayed 'n suited stole my sister's
skin a thorn weld the only three instructions (bur
ning in the corner, stone a burns, lump clam. or the
well "bloomed. stipulation pole in flames "form"
come tell it me! the truth be corn teocalli or your
slippers. puddle blood. the path combs, a knot tlaloc
fire yr hot hand groping in the gravel wire you schem
less scheming glanced into the fog, up

De parture

clam hole said. rapt month ou ou cleaver in the hall
like sand. tree lamp or your trip loam muster wash
it you? "or" calamity a singer moment "planned
b"read over-chewed and in your pocket bleeder: nay
customer like a rancid ham "ney" flute. stand cold,
clay? re decide and re, all tampered was and all.
was hed nothing like a mouth or crown of spokes "blade
the clock" renewed 'n wasps! dripping down the dome's
trained station loss, "ary the"

Pott ee seat

day climb the faucet wheeze light clam.p orn a ment
al raising arms 'n cliff brine the closet's breeze
liporection. stance connection. and a flow fall
(damply (bent 'n air left yr blanket air's misdi
rection ("pedo" (s tank beneath the chaired kiss
hole really itched lank. flume tome caressed you
o: was need and homed, lapper. watch you chained a
nearly strewn my "g ear"s ladder fault "I was
"back""" flap, stayed 'n froggly hauled a lune (the
center's tark

C ash

stay 'n call, claw; leap crow nifty hat with jewelled
eye the old man smoking. puff yr h alter tar between
yr heads a collar phone I dial ate the skin 'n hair
yr giblets steaming on the. steps rug. like poor
condition gland a trial's eat 'n eat. triple moss
you sneezed! trays of leg the tripe flags! matter
mama coughing you, 'n sags flap flap. thrice must,
retard the haul you "made" lost a sinking log a log.
o chew caw repeat 'n drafty me! slow lump (out's t
ring hauled

S tick y tab le

Stay Down the (phone sand boat and dangler in the
chute bare you re turned yr bruise "lame hole"
inna. draft through you behind phew! mot mot "flutey"
said you sot splat. down. drowsy on a reef hot swell
a mud, beach, floating ham just, you and, and...
"flare the hall the Loop the fuzzy sandwich under
fridge sun slot beneath yr grey shutter (storm and
heat stay down yr dirt slick with mayo rice 'n mag
gots clouds, foam, edge

Ee ee

gut home. the drain land, scorched yr pants 'n labile
foundry in the hamper Ed ify congestion like a wind
ow looming in a vacant. field inspect the larynx
crusty chains swallowed belts blood, yr band's//cone
of shit the mall gleams its exzemas oozing through
yr shirt walking backwards. gniklat. looks the same
a pointy turds. sdrut claims yr phalanx bloat the
flood you. ate heel. dusty flames swirling through
yr seat allow a, bacon fold! the wired thigh you
waited weighted, facedown on yr plate. a laundry!

Ah ant erior

can a dome the hall you wrassle loosely itchy in
decisive like a bean rat curled frosting under
side yr chairseat “thoughtless farting” what a leaf!
bean raft you were toothsome blunts. carried scar
away, dark dank ‘n. locks lost redoubled washed yr
dip hole, *whole* reunion where you ass“whole” cake,
mean ‘n fat pearled with flossing? why why, tumesence
salad clear ‘n rings the temple falls. off ‘n mumbles!
(worshipping the socks here here was clasping cheeks
‘n all

Ad d it

blang yr. toe nest you traded thinly reach for. me
at the nail wall//snot//smears back at. m.e. leaks
'n calms the walker, "engorgement" moans "vacation"
leans scabby o'er the shopping cart 'n sang 'n clot
'n: deep feet "'n rougher washer" hand stuffly
thrusting knew yr rotor cuff clam. "calm" hah.
speared beneath the seat was blaster home na g eek
an y name yr motor bloods. "mirrors" my handle
greasy with a hotdog bun the clock "sink" inside
yr paperwait yr shoe yr brimming toilet ya!

Coat licues

play hall, the flat dog skulls behind yr door a
drain heaves breath flipping book yr pants fly
tripled rain inside yr writing arm plain hall the
dog door burns//hat gate//eated through yr knob
bright wit shit "look" yr damp fly writhing arm
like sand intestine coats of name you trade ham
skull behind yr skull dam dome whiffle whiffle.
lapping topic. seethe yr water gifts. nam tone
yr fray shirt licksy licksy reef me heel so's "I"
kin "say" all the (slathered dog yr day skirt

Coat licues

corredor de juego, el perro plano calaverea detrás de
tu puerta un dren jadea respiración libro capirotazo
tus pantalones vuelan lluvia triple en tu brazo de la
escritura corredora llanura la puerta del perro se quema//
portal de sombrero//comelonido por tu tirador brillante
co mierda "mira" tu mosca mojada brazo que se retuerce
como arena intestino capas de nombre cambias el jamón
calavera por detrás de tu calavera dique domo soplado
soplado. tópico lamido. hervir tu regalos agua. tono
nam tu camisa se rae lamelón lamelón arrecífeme tacón
para que "yo" pue "decir" todos los (perro embarrado
tu falda tu día

brea kin

brain’s foam the. glanded hall retrieve you huh,
favored L abounding corners where yer paws “pause”
a blander motion “or contain” my sever ation che
wing off the sill a rancid banger “flaw flaw”: yr
sticky bowl of milk ‘n Gangrene Flute, o spinning
rafter swell for me you tick! cold fall drift
mouldy like yr bun drain’s phone my phone, kinda.
stickulated. pun gent. for am the dand led bah llum
uh “uh” came ‘n coughed an hour at the door was too
much meat still. reaching *through* the form recall,
like *caves*! the table in

Rap t

yer cello torn across the sand o sacks o' shells
'n tampon inserters reams you f lushed when I de
tailed the mensual steam beneath my shirt lamp
mouth cramped tacky south 'n clear Mist Mist.
cradled your my head de tachment curdled eyes be
held. the cong. río smoke sinking past Temuco
blankets in the woods thick with rain yr who spores
a (hand (gum tracks I c left be hind quartered all
de lections from the pore mirror "butt but" yr
chained wrist swerves "yer pillow" "mu d in haled"

Gaz e ro

pare the boots-clown, p low. the lace floats 'n
stalls ra pt ow main contention yuk "or c lap"
fall chewed yr hoppyface today a raft of tiny
logs swirls before the flus h you. s wallowed in
a songs hit "flywheel" back-compaction. reef (er
smile you fried tongue di lection cluster your-mud
pall. compare the Mud pl ant, dome flow. eat or
eat you scald tripping toward the pearly shaft o
grimy fog ! a s meer utters under you no matter
deep no blat her ranges in the road you stut ter
minal a clot hopper "hop per

Loc kd ress

name the cOmb raTher can fOrm a meant her crashing
through the closEt less sPatter on my gLasses there
I twirled, badly combed but formless spent fall
leaking or (a closet) glass walled drippy foot you//
chew the fog clay drilled 'n twirled my blutwurst
shiny teeth ("TV") or bready door behind the icy
street thick like churning clay black salt clumps
loud crows the//door a "spLinters cLuster" my vacant
mouth a drill or hamsters (tiny meAt like all re
Wards) flat you-lens-mind savored with's incision
tines across "yr slabby skull

Ra nout

stay stay the ice win dow heaves in claw claw torn a
hole yr brain clotted and de tailed roofing left
burning heaves in slime born corn syrup fills yr pan
ts gets slow haw. tale o' faucets woof woof "slippery
knob" your *reeking*-cans, formless like//a closet in
spaghetti water mumble pees, yr dust too "clear" Mr.
Slabber trained to steer beneath o mattress flakes
cave the hall outside, yer *tumbled* sneeze, dormantic
"like a chain" crusted (wit's lost lunch the ice fog
streams (haul

N air

fist tub eager frame you soggy and intentless like a
vacuumed hall wip. ed if I my fog-thought sticky ham
left out in the sleet like stillness at the breakfast
table's bandaged wrist a moth a mother er "implacable",
spoons. bitter ed a bowl or you, mister "thud's the
name" stroke a blackened ball "out in" the street a
cave you flushing in, "flushing" pretty sight but
(crushing you, sore relentless stunt or flack my
arm or (dripping fall

F eet

'n clamber drip regardless knob 'n hair you spat
across the freezee driveway slot slot the stain ball,
bat me drum concussion's "rift" of plugs 'n air you
sat across the grapefruit rinds a glistened heap 'n
tongue. where yr shirt of bandaids, move it *with your
skin* o rage-a-day calendap rotes re re! (grinds and
flutters like your soup o chortle fruit blunt masseuse
in spite (cave nail lap cooky hang yr head 'n "stool
there" glistens in yr cup "that hamster" reef an call
me through the window where I wait ignore the (fea
thered ladder

O se ano

por legaña sand a rain a plosiva cucu racha de
tu. telef o bajo mi (torcerme he tu taco n ota vale
suma mierda ("hachón") lo más cor tenido alborada
gris-azul mi blan co bla nco: ráfagas de "cab rito"
(camisón de lluvia-rubber nido almeja knob cadera
me o llama cómo almohada como. instantáneo y nada
por la isla y galleta ("gallo" o) pain eh? los pelos
de aspir ina actitud tu ojo leído tu ojo neg activo
lo que flota como rueda no mercurio: (espedo (cola,
niebla lam bo

Up u p

nor t reach fer me yer flat cave writ, “claw”
lamp or “tiny float” er clumb left ‘n g razing
cross t my back like noon shambles, flushed the bag
of chips you s aid yer flaco comb activo (“speech
slave”) drained across my s lacks like pak o’
chicken legs’ blood soaked diaper. tu ne h and, yr
cluster-vestigation it ch ea ch, the stand o’ s
heep paw me “p lease” please oh. *really* nekkid in
my s kinless shirt, *instigation* was’t? mud ‘n
sleep? clam clam pt

S ter

co lut her bliss et che wink at yr wrist he was yr
boom bum choffed. the "black ice the" espejo with a
nail through's shruggle in the bathroom kinda rub
less, uh "robe". waf t er claw noun yr pelo, reefs
of sinks and rearview mirrors ("bums") your swimming
out to see dog p addle whifflers in the mutter flow
maw. no'm bray or suit e sui te tip flabbering on
the bathmat like an ear syringe "ring ring and tant
"ilize" (n uc your s tar you r fa r se

La m al

c lame hun ch at turn b lack to c ling like fauce t
c rust les in yr darken ed bat hroom wak ened n ode
rum p. wak ‘er h all ‘n s lumped yr bag o’ wet ling
uini’s c rankcase oil stun (t claim you l earned
ding ‘n (“dat”)e widening backwords sty “’n stark”
while you were. implode l’histoire you ee ee. k fl
pp! a pen alty far yr bray yr B Ray m atted kite
concussion “f lat b ag c hips rust ling in yr” se
at a kinda vacushirt a th ought be hind yr br eaching
hair do do m

Tre pination

bean foam or was yr nostril? back words a and
loose full robe bath you ex pectored nostril
("words") labelled and cor-stained-was. loosely
flipped against the wall blamp lamp expectant.
like "retention" flipped it off off the limp
splotched *rug* you wore that splap: cree c r ee
was glass ("limp 'n splot" spit fast you ate *ate*
that leg room rug, several years, seething in the
hamster squealing hamster in yr bean wheel's shiny
little leg (cor leg

Er gonomic

the FORm cLAW leaked did dit wAved above the HolE
you jigg led. in tail ed the heavy flaw Heaped
outside my sole ("sticky") wristed gum the nose I
chewed like tougher. boarded up the lake debris 'n
"lists" you wiped yr wit h. ee ee stuffed up there!
the clacking nap flake or "bean rat" was, snuffing
back again again a chanchre bore: dreamed that buzz
that fIst? oh nodder at the vacuum "cleaner hose"!
(strained above the at the stool "hoarded" (cancel
lation, canc

Ton sure

yr cLuttered edge yr ("clutter-edge" like, "combed the
hills "kneed the lease yr "blat slan der com vection
and a folded cage inside yr chest "the bills" peed re
lentless so yr ambulation fodders mighty toothy for a
loaned itchment or a stage of flutter cross yr neck 'n
pamper aspirgate yr finger dink dink. *re* time. or lever!
sorta lip o suction-elevation pig high onna pole ("boss")
...linger 'n stale, so yer fraying "looks like hair"""""""

P last

really nap the mud ("salary") tripping in ("toward")
hamb one you rattle in the muffled what yr chest
leak leak. *twist* floor, the ran, *blown* nabber of the
loss receipt a nibble and the *rouster* tune core o'
travel through yr hair like stifled (hamsters in yr
armpits) tossed salad at the driver vroom. release
that *gravel* handfull o it's glassy. e pleur back-o-
the-bus that one eye nails you to the rant. "flaunt
you flaunt you FEET FEET" lurk 'n presidented like a
hat 'n axe. You (Gleam

Ne w ork

saw tooth cough you glistened at the train a cluster
drag across yr arm stunned fight ‘n sleeve flagellation
(“long wipe”. the “flag” throne or. “blister cud a loo
se farting through yr shower, handle ruckus “moon a
bove the streaming” bowl yr stark candle was nor “luck
gland eat yr tripe. tripe. them sallow spiggots on the
senado floor (“sputum”) stuck-like, “leach out through
yr hole wafter, “arm less””””” bust respire a shattered
wrist clocks the tracks Gleam, agAin

Exc usado

dime ball clutched the disks dinged out across the
urinous mens ("library filled with tape and matches
("slime hall ("throat lunched 'n drips tree, caul.
blinked across the pill? the furnace quivers and I
clanged yr fall that board er toil et? drain slants,
clogged with peanuts nu. a river strains yr "foot
flack, tritely muttered what, madderisms, mordicried,
musky like. that log you runted. flay m flay m! hut
ched above the s ink you (bun sorer then; o you fla
bber knocker, See!

Do mitus

sta ined the flo or amp led stancer youp encilled
ary g loom without the sky pen nood les sleep yr
st inking hand b luddites "you" were g rainy o 'n
itchy. faced yr sock pole writhing in yr pants er
boom. ripped out the sl ime ham, yr stud ded rift,
was hed c rush? ed yr b ready list 'n chewed 'n
chewed strained the buried door you d ay, or *brings*
my slap hush focussed on yr brush. ah instead you
grew! (pile I spelled back dimming in the flo oded
(clos et packed with (think wrists

Ro w r ow

dome of flame the udder car glamp ns tear yr nape
that fLoat he ap s kreeling bridely ankle ant ant,
sewn the same cluttered arm 'n damp near tape ("duct")
cloaked, yr fleet ass, timely sank. clamp yr stomach
dereliction and a tidal, tidal spew what. you enjoyed
in snot rags a final carg o *true* aspirina. clot joy.
look up the flame an "aeresol" yr drive correction's
sagging lake (nor leaks!

Y ank le

turd 'n shovel, bean hat flutters in garage fluoresence
("flatulence" came 'n) drably stubbled past the foaming
birdseed nip nip. or tree sand the roof steams wha ta,
nabber! backside heard 'n double flabbed the, utters
savage ob solescence stabber ("name" 'n glandly troubled
faster faster. groans you pees clip or clip. hand woof.
the shadowed bean clank behind yr shattered "shoplight"
was a pin. a pin! kinder sea my: (lips or lice...

Fl ap f lap

"wha ta" me ing the fLaming pOle 'n rusty nOdules
balling ouT the bAck wer e galLing out the back's
id le heavink cRust o user-name de tale me "talKing
lad"der! trust the talking ladder tp roll o' skin
you text. protext the sadder meatus left or. left
rendition of the mines beneath yr flag beneath yr
flagging monster toot, wRithing like the grIlle be
neath yr shirt. shirt storm. yr sleevey face! yr
sievey face o windy pole...

W rite it chy

kneader oil I need yr boil ing caus tive hallway
"cost defective" hallway off yr back 'n reeling,
reeling coughed back there 'n left yr sung toot
sung tout all night. reef reef o empty snacker
sags outside yr faucet clawed was he, claude 'n
stooled. (stool *sandle* falls, bled outside the)
drain outside the cranial convection cursive,
thirsty like contraction of yr loudest phone!:
loud est foam or oil (oil!

Na pie

oil's trilled 'n aeresol detachment from yr bloody
lap yr bloody lap ping behind the ear o stave yr
hat in stave yr hat like socks 'n matches soaking
in the toilet toilet cloaked with yr behind the
looming methane curtain curtain of yr shifting
towels twisted down yr pantsleg down yr pantsleg
like a roll of sticky nickels and a flag a flaco
dragged outside the clown outside the Clown. rusty
rusty. and the sticky rustle of those wings

S atsa t

the *triple* shrug the. tank flakes drifting near the
drain the drain detailed with numinance a shift of
muscle. shifty mussels in yr asshole ("asshole"
flavor of the) mouth like lapcheek soup 'n mould
scummed like sunked TV o soaked 'n soaked the.
blank TV er yr behind a starter face (er yr) (behind
the bowl a looping mirror a soup. where you scratched
yr skull 'n scratched yr skull you gave that riddled
shrug that *riddled* (tub of

So: re alb u men tal lak e

Ne: ar t ea f ish a l l á na dis tan cia

Fog: rand om bli go ng ng

Na: t e ur e mi a baj o der ma ma l

Phon: kee s may gn at tri ti ti on do lat e

Hom: in e ap or ia llig n (g nn g

Pa: n demo nlea p yhor rea c t

Do: mi ney bor e all is tt t

Vio: la g am bas tan k ast a b

Yo: ke l p eg g la ns ept ic k

Cla: w mid yia pp lic able d sk y

No: r te arro r ice me n t mot h

Po: re tal i at e eet ha mb ean

W heat h air

fall ink off the tab le livre lèvre laid back out side
the chair split tea, or bald. "think often" fable, lièvre
flayed 'n sacked besides yr hare spit "pee" tajine de
motes mot tled yr eyesite streaming pillow "like a sink"
you. cared 'n cleaned those sticky notes (sot) shed, *dry*
you, sightless cleaning of, the pond drill. stared right
through yr clot hes, time 'n rab bit id enteric entered
in, yr spin pan comb slime "he's go t" o know to no. the
(coughy table (laid ur head

Ste am at tire

leaker hall you warmly scent inside yr coat uranus roast
the *damp* tang lop plan g ent eritis but yr spoke. whirled
'n *whirled* dinkly!//forceps table gleams 'n bloods the
hairless//drink gland you ("bloat") starkly in the wall
the wall arp. ar p ending-glooms the coast below yr swell
peed far out 'n writheses down 'n writheses, kinda wavy
ladder in yr cheeks' cleat, swarmy pants yr claw like's
(law or creamy shorts o sags regaling! (floa ting cloth
e s o com b e com b

Ham mer

glint the nail hand o cough! *try* de rail, pleasure-sit
know bleach yr hammer-head was sweetly rusted and a
third. combusted. achy achy bland. trim each clot or,
deeply now. ("*try* to, measure-wallow//lipostructure,
clave) the//meaty storm 'n crust. gate. leach yr moss yr
mount spoke fadly cross the tab le sphere le ad terse
visor ("plate" juts) up again said the light "stammer"
noose a floating fat derangement cud you pout? name name
but crack. or scratch the clavo just a key stinking
to the bottom. justa (gleam knee)

Run d oor lay

blaze yr hammer or was wet? tape the woRm fOam lethal lap
a sty me'd lighter cap yr *soaker* fan yr, soaker fan er
daze beneath the table likely marsh a liquid march across
the kitchen like those squid yr fury threw yr fury threw
against the windows with a pleasy squelch a squelch. yr
tepid hat contention left, yr mighty labile. or was stub
bled, stubbled was and leechless was yr door? yr door was
hair unswept? I was dampness counter-veiling, outside the
mime. so where I *wet* my crust, crust 'n hammered in yr
blaze

D ran ka bit

slap yr" hall 'n crum ble nd the ninnies in yr pocket
gash o phone held the crumbs left in yr. hair gore
("spinning hat" a) gate a floor yr (face? gleams with
vaseline squeezed through a sock. past the doors was.
slow and heaving. "heaving//drainly" caustic light
the//lumpy nail apron "corn bones" left yr teeth you
"splashed 'n leaned"? tepid phone but sunk hammered
with a rock oh please! striped with rash er rash.
"blow seething lint"? or list was lost key lost beet
lost (tripe; forms the axle's "itchy feeling

Nigh t rem ens

dat" ur a blow ner vitus g lance the g ate reTention
floaters! nob o can, 'n sloshy. can you gel ate? the
trace f lunky gal e liver "liebre" heaps across the
yard like candor nodes metastasizing in yr stark damp
bed. loss of clothes. "foam rat" colitis and an itch
an ick. the lever bubbles and decays so heavy d rink
a bas kit tall fome leaking out yr head a cabb age
sludge ee center sky's no de da ance dis per sal ad
offal... ben eat h yr plate nuous 'n... quivery,
sopp ing sleeve stuffed in yr pants a "thought you c
lad... (sha key d rain...

N od d or

stare the hall gak gak the lunger flew but you de
strayed, the. clamp. drooly in the sensitivity work
shop "Mr. Drooly" huffed beneath the table slack a
fauce t ank le spew back yr head gate aw. chew the
cable in yr pants thc blank (blank .a needle only
mud you lurk? cl am ph on ora g listen s in the morn
ing's log float ("clogger", so yr hand must, eat the
entry was a *warning* was, ah my nap glare the door
you shuddered in! steep 'n slapping, cloudy rivers
in yr hair...

See p

my itchy closet where you sit ‘n st alled ‘n. it’s it’s
glean ham purr the c offer lap intide, yr sleep, snail
it claws, stretchy “faucet” hair you’s. pit the lens
it’s, called why and you the. furry-side yr heap o’
nails. aw now, claim. or dot dot ring ‘n liv er wurst
noun un der floppy-table where you foun der tail, up
‘n. up the slat hered wall flat ‘n “stair” heel dam age
it’s yr trousers even, sputtered out the doorway port er,
a pat tered out ‘n sop ping in (ner sl eep

Aut osa alte r

yr preyer foam or I was g lad's g land .date I k lept
you a te back on yr preyer dome a cir cle and I c ame
doritis "after" fore, after forceps or .a key lave
write tamped amount to hoses, mounted hoses to yr foyer,
fuer was hed it? lake 'n Lake like clapped. .the too
must, must too fore compaction .wash it itchy or?
.rabbit ladder or a rabid ladder leaking like .your haul
name ring, ringing dust cu pola antes de mi dicho: dicho
es piral o really baggy .(leapt behind the car

Fa n ned a he ad

uh hairy flaw low, flaw low den damper sore yr spoon,
yr spoon wasp I 'n dry. thigh dry yr heaver, trope
.trope list the lamp convection, vector of .a noose
spout a. ramp's pouting toward the g land d rink
landed drinks and thorns along the channel .channel
long a core. yr housing dereliction like a gash in
side yr leg, inside yr leg was falling-gesture .cla
wed along? (drip (d rip oh napkins in your "sanitary-
hat" your hat reduction like a funnel! (like a funnel
plunged, into yr h airy s law

Di vision lu me

the spork the tween the lack ‘er gate thaw the fork be
side yr door ‘n spat s .it ram a way ga lore a *stream*
flab.flabber .taste it pile. a cave the. nor relenting
no nor while the cor relation was nit .t ame f law? c
rust de bacle rut you che wed (*nearly* game, but) writ-
dust .oh snore re daction! cleaver hole... the shave the
.sped defied, your hammock like a salad salad mould
(inside you, rear .socks me try, and true re jection out
the plate off .“redo the speckled night...

sTall

the mIst the
hAll the
cLam t
he
P

Activo

tHat boAt you
wrEath erd yo
ur liNe T cou
Gh

oh ou

Le ap d own

cabled “ham” d rank you drank. a lessor cliff noon pud
dled on the table where the table lift your. brine eye,
reeked a while or “while” across the snow a cross the
snow - like blink - your lumber raft tine the rafter
ticking. eat by eat .the hole thing caved and outer sand
wich sandwich or a roof bleat bleat. glass and crime.
the vapor wet the va por collar washed in steel was money
and a septic shoe you shoed so roughly? why’s the matter?
lease you greying in the closet closet drowned inside the
roast .dripping off your chair your hammy “chair”

Se ad rizzle

s pot dam hole the reef sing s pouts of rising see things
of clos er sky er slot s and was drinking in yr sleep ice
s lopes grin the deep hall lies in rain yr . dampest pock
et crawls "with" maggots? jujubees? the dor mant coin flags
oily mantis and a cliff yanked free... yr pee sighs yr.
tide lockets drains yr .wallet spills its hair clouds writ
he still than. bare mouthe .the krill injection eaten all
smutz left yr (sectioned eel in(side yr (skull chest drone
a s in king dull swell you. try 'n dry yr "foamy things"
(sloppy bell a .top the peeled hill

Ga te di me

lum b read smoking in the base meant re tection of yr
ra don t ally me ‘n lumpy yr .red face stroking was yr
“meat de”jection out the side do or a s cuffing down
the alley to ward yr muddy river sigh(phon faucet put
yr mouth on “co razón” (sluffs down inside yr .bloody
sleeve a .tip out ‘n po ur - c louds ‘n handles -
lifts out tu bo ca gato were yr pants? I re ached yr
sand wet beneath the sla b ow l rocking there a (dance
o loca! louder than an ant a d rifts a .sLobber to ward
the sLammer-wall (low or c rumbling (“stymy”

Lac words

as ass re tard the mud he aving in yr sideyard trip le
timing toward the aim's retention aim's re demption off
yr cr adle slat a long and bloody splinter splinter
sang you sailed outside the gland ag land ululating in
yr bathtub like a drink a drink of wood and pacifiers
sticky with yr plans yr plains of grocery bags crack
ling in the breeze you're filled with foaming chain re
mover chain removal mi pistola dripping oil down yr leg
yr leg I g lazed beneath the table at beneath the table
bright with ants with .ants

La p eyes

sleet thong 'n drift slyly aft the ball name thin grisections
was a ladder wasp a ladder drained beneath yr feet mite. tea
run down yr leg yr downy leg washed with light (tub (dent the
sand form the formal sand gashed or was yr river? meat meat.
the twitching sandals or your looping. teeth your looping
teeth I bowed before, your liver pallor was an empty sheets
empathic sheet or blindness like a floor. the icey rung neck
you climb. or climbed my neck like seborrhea like a truce.
your door. your door mitosis turning side my sleet

He ap t

bread silence. reef reside your doll re mote control 'n
glassy deign tool. yr red. sigh gash deep outside the
floor yr twitching on. oh fleet. the tied induction ripe
a slammer ("snore" yr) itching faucet and yr kitchen suit
yr dome raisin burns or .leaf the ham mer .contravection's
foam 'n spray. warshed a triple doubt or Pete Petro rolled
beneath the bed asleep a "wobbly" trick like sputtered
"lunch" blank rabbits and disection cuts yr haunch you
moon above the table rubbers crum ble hike a shadow napkin
(spoon, glove, stroking turd your thrashing feet ("astride...

T one lin e

glaz ed n chi lly" .use da te mpl eaf uh *.link* for "once" for once 'n bla zed a cross the wind shielded nothing o r azed me? grazed me er spiny tails re lented dently dently rended like yr teeth re gurged, regurged com passion like yr slip .pry phonelines stagn ant fart beneath yr blank et blanket .strew yr sonogram yr .tied 'n true yr dried 'n true in jection or was re? de piction of the clearing-wheel clearing drill and hand. writ writhe the. timbre splayed a .coustic freezing and your rustled fawn a (rustled yawn yr "facing f layed

Sta red oor

dra ped al loss yr for ehead an eel a conger up respect
for m eat re spect for me at all .intentions snide or
.roughly samp led tout. you stamped it out 'n rightly
but yr face was gleaming gle aming like yr "face" yr
cutting .trumped 'n phoned like trus sed be neath the
so fa ben eath the sof a pool .mud yr was a ."drain"
a laundry think .but think re diction think a congeries
of faucets faucets like yr "running-sore" a window to a
moon ."a moon all" right a tab le o yr "lips were draped...

Mun dial

room ahaul a bade morn a bath. yr muddy pants a current,
cur rent dayed behind a mind you .double oh a drip a d
rip behind the chair beneath your lamp al amp you reading it
your anus rice above the chimney rise above and narrate
air. err-narration whiffy. feet 'n falls. tore *off* the
floating "log" the floating .shine-face sleeping flour
in the wind a flower were you winded? bobbing in the tub
a bobbing-track a fortress and a misted .misty wheezing
on the roof a moon a mon

Ron do

st reake d oubt a
sl ant
                    der a
              WHOLE-lisper

derma “d ance”

(loom)

Cave

C row goo

chaired the gland foam cream re duction? tree p eat the
clang felt (yr behind o bad inage I ate yr hair! grand
dome above the river irritation "slacking throat" door
door. thrip infestation. more clean sound yr bowels
"bowls" past the cage cages tastes yr liver coughs real
loud. yr lip screen yr *flutter* jumping stance o writhing
neck before the island! stacks of goat a snore yr "pine
barrens" flagged with plastic bags yr "leaning-dance"
was "sitting-jitters" was my pants spattered with your
sneeze spring's chain "inaction" (slim ey c raw

Anguage

the storm the float the stammer night headless body twit
ching in the mud a stack of legs you slept against like
logs and sleep yr fogs ‘n forms like rice smeared on yr
face and nose the zit the ingrown stare “contactual” clu
bbed the slack o’ rubber-books was every word was was
itching in yr “ranch chips” cud slump. sl ant d eep off
the r eeking be d pee p ee sho re f lame. yr “clammy-kite”
dips ‘n bucks blood-smeared ‘n hammered sight of “rain?”
g nat gnat leaks. yr lumpy socks was “was”, a kinder o
ffal hog you loved. rubbed against ‘n nude, “new k new”
o “grimy-gland”

Sub duction

score's groan yr. grown ladder, reefer than my hand. yr
reek yr reach. so bite my ankle slab or. contabulation
aster glows, inside yr chest an habanero. chile pressure,
climb the sack drapes yr head 'n guess the dust induction-
alley. flicker-talk and gas, or spillage. steak rungs yr
feet o faster still. stay undressed, fill the cages, dry 'n
flutter. deeper than a door you moat, motes 'n dingle-
berries, bury all those coughing pages. bladder-bright.
yr beach face blooms, a shiny acne "skin's hams"

H our s lope s

the trail o' form recedes o mitey clam bor e alis drippy
with yr spa stick-bladder climb the slope of stones "scree".
breather-valve yr table seethes a "sprightly-fan" or fart.
list. yr dribbly-office blinder than a mirror my cud o. the
cloudy-table I could drink, but drinked heavy boots. "bright
dust" yr blood glance. louder fable than the news was even
tailed outside the binding. "mindless" babble, "brook" no r.
and the itemization was, contusion should of rising shingled
tower. "o pen fire" said, o

Natt erbe ds

stap le fract al comita tus nal gas .dra ped across yr
h air fo am bled thinly in my s tool .wurst the wear g
rout flame a round the b are you .dang led oh ,d ribbly
pool inside yr .head g rain y an swer ves tal co litis
am .pled no n ame nor f arting cutely was ?you simper"
slimy stew ".but Bach's worst fall or .fugue dis play
'n gegen t ape is lit like .yr liver mice paté 'n vest's
all chun ky with" .lungs er "words tomadas en .tu cor
redor 'n spe wed bes ide yr knee yr .flop py kn ee

S well am

n ape blo od bright ah ha a .sha king tow el lago d ran k
‘n sloshed to ward bed .time s ticky l eg g o mud plate
deep t high yr s wallow !mice)red loss the(hall drilled
‘n smokey kicked my ankle loose o .follow hole the .sleep
crain ial ow d rain inside yr short s unk shoe ‘n ho se .a
hacks ecution rice ‘n larva dance !a beach chunky was hed
up books yr hollow finger c lam intention .itchy ?pee
back-back yr l umpy th ought huh .strip st rip one fewer
nose a car mine g ape !so to eat o sweaty hook yr .acid
re lux and a b rain...

S prey yer

r aw han ded was hed out to see m y f ace rea imed at"
me "yo seet he mar maw can died h ash in aned !o Ned ther
g ates pees dry)m ist o' free dome(langour ,lengua mi
mapo mundi ,coatl ,stay slow eye ,in brains upon a pill ow
sneeze d phone the chanchre blend a reek-arc hive r so re
p alm leached out" floater "ha bit .na ked like a bean er
r at foam" bend over here " cheese 'n bunnies ,r aft
across the delta's swirling se wage dip dip 'n sp latter
day yr scaly poll a week of glans ejection .fly yr nape o
muck contains(yr flicking-wall

Dust f laws

s law a slee ping you ,creamy f olds a drippy in the
sheet ts like smiles ‘n bluntcracks filling all yr c laves
like dark like light lac tation glee glee .yr dairy arm
awrithe yr fan between yr legs” apool “my(hand pane stomach
,brighter than a claw your deepest leaning off .told a rip
ping in yr feet yr)piles of grunting sacks(a chilly lake
‘n barking” action “f lame f arm arrives yr span m a dream
of eggs ‘n drool ,yr same story I .was sleeping in the floor
a water ladder mindlessful a s warm you)guess(my gland it
was or)snore a leaking ,was h wa sh

Soo n so on

flame hole your flame whole corn pain was py lad der in
yr eye lame snow I .stuffed my pocket whiff gak gak naus
eous in yr .tree clot a dentition lush with algae and yr
clauses !lick the sunset sweetner dry with donuts and I
growl uh .crawl writ aphids toward the rung dine c lap,
show ers lips lip my .driving lung lid dead "occulation"
ticking .in yr fat yr .towel drool I nap ped itchy faucet
I be .held my Mouth rudder than yr .butt key)cloud I(
lost my .other-smell my)flooding ditch

Dent al den t o

d rank hall .the tee ming mi torn asol wilting in the
)basement ham(mer de)louche screws ejected pocket s
laps against yr waste yr .drank ball buried in .yr face
d rips ,form a .doll crackled in the sun you .uh ,stam
mer a .loop case or I a spector lessened spit .blooms
inside yr c lock sea foam meer .sham ?done you the !seep
ing wristful *lolls* ?time to say .it c lusters like yr
.scabby shanks all .*buggy* with the seeds p hew a .list
moans like you re placed it)spackled like .yr eggs yr

Rea p re ap

t rained to s tall and mice buried in yr bin yr rags
dreaming in the base meant to skim ly coninflate but
.traded off 'n all com batent liked, *was* it you ?ble
ed bleed 'n .tiny flavors)bin 'n bags ste(aming drinkly
wash yr bite my .blade rum ,pled for re solution but's
crust see thing yr .burning pants a .crawl inside yr face
'n *save* 'er seeds the deepest stairs .think rice sprawls
doubtside 'n flames' a sign .o' rafter breaking !breathe
volution dance 'n dry)yr sank thing dome s it)sigh s

Nob k lean

t ray the dips tick's c rawful lath er and you eat each
'n b awl treeless where you .mons tremens sticks a shad
ow or .leap a side you .call Steamly mr. after trace .yr
teeth-slide f loor flo or glaring up the siding *want* to
talk .no trace yr d awning snore my c link my clin k g
land sump or r eaching in the black be breath you ,crowning
)"crow" a(type o' mortal-form s er face-sack ,all misty
was you was an streaked with ,caulk adrink ,my mightly
neighbor rights through you I I .opposed my doubt

Tri jecta

steam cone “one” damp ‘n listening to yr final chalk.
dust lamp, ‘n brimming caves you. chunk hover’s sample
steam, you dried yr lip yr spinal caulk ‘n flood up
straight tho foam ed, was. the think stays, drippy and
“besides” wash kinda stunk I, flavored with my Crisco
Kid my lengua lengua what .you sprayed, me vasoline
,cular traded for the narrow .hall .me stomping fidgets
o linguini lid my hat)”vascular”(an culeando .twice
sunk three spaded spat yr placa :tree perched was ,thick
with sauce smoke ‘n .lists crime lists floatage lists
gargle rising in the

Me mer e

tiny eye shoal the .mater reel sit kak ‘n dies .thin
grime a face you off the dock back .treble itching’s
sore yr ladder smoking like a “faucet whore” some
“guest” merely dithering at the stormdoor go away feets
,one grim dime between yr teeth cheap grin ‘n .lather
bread shirt a heavy mirror sky sky .o trade my itching
sand you sleeting in that chair yr stapled wind across
the floor ‘n madre fish afloppin sock “connection”
all-in-order an a swirl an .eddy like ,yr falling wrist
yr . cloaca smelts ,slowing brushing out

D ark c rust

,stand and snore)the cave key hot ‘n limp a grain di
rection tri ponential(” ponencia “mouldering in the
file your .bland drinking ,poring o’er the huffing-
text your headache’s water ,wheel dama(“ harm ”)aster
tinkling next the pork egg gland ‘n lucent-quenched I
,grew yr fall ,drained ‘n held yr red” halter “)lumpy(
like yr faster heaving .brea the shore ‘n ruff le de
fecation-folder carried far ‘n wide a tal es man dalo
mantic !all a sheaf o air ,drenched !yr tongue twit
ching in a box ,sand sparkling ,kinda kitschy souvenir(
brus hed yr feet off

P ath or u

stained ‘n hammy ,lichen flap b oiled juice ‘n flop-steak
,s t raining o’er the stool yr hand le left ,age of coughing
like a ,lander in the bow l ring ring .race of sewage in yr
RAFT pondorrhea)“dripping ears”(‘n clotted rake you slept
with ,trace of drool among the chips .d rank socks ‘n coi
led inside yr” shorts “s lope th ick ‘n d rumming” like a
bell?//drab floaters at the wall yr//knee sank ,bloody an
protrusion-lobbing ,was yr apex-posturation” prostrate-
sand “o floods yr crotch :a cancellation and a hinge bright
with moss)lain out beneath the bridge black pants

Ra no ut

chained a lone rug ha t able aped with dregs of .door
phone ,aw fulla term ites like yr noose yr runny belt
c link clin g the trip le song le sunk)across yr s
ticky f loor s poor(blade me down .aimed for your re
tention I ,chewed yr heave n w reath was s pelt 'n spilt
ground ago .was truced 'n b om bed ,c abled to de stain"
my "ratio cination)"strewed"(outside my" sound ".bud
dub 'n corp ses inking in a field .you" silt "you bred
insection ,knives 'n came rata loosely burning .leaps of
all your ,tri-impaction drinked...

Rar es nout

b lang f loat you ucked d rain b linking in the wall
was ter mites ?do you and n eatly s tutter .reef the
chain regret the hol ding to yr ,losses close ts ts an
flood-taled .yr ut tear mace rations knife ,fol ded in
yr slee ve p ,rice-heavy ,was yr dipping in that" faucet-
place "trouble rub ble .ape the raft you .crisis-beery
and demaned ?just think just" think "s lip b urned the
shirt you blo at !ease o r ease !//twit ching roast//'n
cacavera c rackling" mice-full "nice 'n truthy but de
saned)"sanditation"(getting go the garb age bag...

C rag n et

near the damp lock. your clavi cord or rain shaft//icey
flame retention in your//"fault", was rip bled, kinda
toothsome for the stipulation that, dripping in yr argued
foot "my" siezure and a chord of gutters like a ham sand
wich "in yr lap" a coil of thrilling caulk. lum pectomy
your. fulsome boil 'n rudder like a "cram" yr up. he he
you your//soilage plumes against the sky 'n oil, tanks
burning "like a gland sandwich" held your cock et key
(drained the calf, "lucka luck"

Cam a lock

bomb stool the half you leapt left gagging up the street
or was down was trepination sore Mochica poring in a pot
"trepiration" for the fire a nag. a crag, 'n lopped the
floor tripled como pocas la de men mi tía//sheet glistens
in the rain//tom fool but slept *before* the news slept
"glandular" palm against an eye your. corpination cradle
shaped a duck kak inside yr arm torpedo list was Burphy
Slacks 'n come dido. raze against the score "listen here"
a singulation swarm the TV off but "kinda slurpy" like a
gumi dildo "licked the dampened" grass

Rab bit e

sly ness rain 'n flam bow a guest dispenser why'd you
cleat my face lap click "klik" (guns 'em down the
lunchroom burbling blood soft (track me (blaring eye clam
sunk yr nest protector curst a lash, 'n septic curds be
neath the hood laughing keyboard bright with pancake syrup
eat my face o special horses equus carnivorus tendon lad
der and I "danced", lumber kinda fern in every earhole
waving "I the blender" pee and storage. freezer stars, yr
under hopeless. ha ha ha ha ha time (snakey

De tail de tale

blink blink. trap ped whom ped I yr padness "pad ma ntic"
waiting in the barkinglot beneath the hail hail. meat
entrancement so yr clapping-links 'n antipedal (crazing in
the dark right bombs 'n, cutters-leg, acid roof, yr naptic
roomers stutter lurching up a, reach-stunt, 'n fast yr
attic foot. dry muttered slurping ("closet") breaked away
or "braked". 'n *lobs* renditions of the con-chest "what
you flapped!" thrilling hole yeast tragic. ta tock, *lend*
bit me. or rap ped me hanging socks my Mr. Johnee fists,
crammed outside, crammy in

Mat to gro sso

de ploy de car ious ‘n “drinking” smoker oil a modest
trance ‘n sacked against the wall o you whee “there”
tang tang grunt the (nodding-sore, agreed too much, a
grieved ‘n sloped toward snackfood danced upon yr chips-
bags “pops” enlightment, sprightly so indebted to the
cutup he re versed the shift ‘n crashed into’s foun
dation shat block try this at home re(lented sightless
teeth all ratty with dessert. ‘n snore-soup, linking
back toward’s w hole ‘n sloppy. yr (lips-rag soldly
dripping...

Ear th ro b ial

sh rinkin was ‘n, tabled pratt le ball d rape d yr shorts
but “eye” was all, glaring brown the hall ‘n, gaseous
(“drinking in”) years ‘n years of slaughter “sphere of
corpses” blue ‘n sailing aetheria yr weeping in yr puke
o Melotrauma claw the shades! speech flake the gutted
horses smoulder “houses” loops ‘n, crawls across the bed
I did, too kite too peed too wrapped out tripas a menudo
como hojas poesía book of leguas lenguas castraciones. try
the blister now. marry all the trembling guns or doub led.
!hold me leg ba laba, (“eggs” ‘n...

Flo tee

taste the hammer flauta fit fully drain delays yr .typ
ology and tamped .on down the pout you ,trailed behind
,'n cryogenetics reef you .pulled it on .redounded to yr
phosphorescence ,hiked a crash" intention ",*but* replied
.tres gullas was ,'n pounded through the islands ...with
yr dead mice bowl ...full you quivered like yr face ah
hammy was !)bed to tell(and breaded for the boats ...las
islas llaman ,llamean ...falda day last night and ,awful
drenched I)floated not ,es connection ,ex(crescent ly

Upp erware

bowl I draped ,with" yr excrescence "likely gashlight
and I glistened in yr windowcrack ...soggy towel the
basement floor ...with my slacks 'n pasta shredded like
the calendar I put my meat days on o pork slam chock
but//you were splashing when I left ,leaping intumescence
with the bread 'n" sky like water rushing ",trade with
me .forking sands ...that" bright blue face ")indenture
,like my oily feet my palms it cupped ,drained in thought
,at least don naide thinner yet than thins ,sore I was
yet supped ,and dribbled on the foil you kept your my
steries in)the

Nu t s law

knacker knacker slide agonic norm all eaten ,was yr sla
ggy hairdo like my rice thorny ?or liposuction through
yr gag rule tried to climb a tree .or what drinks ,the
thick unskimmed was “us” he hoo .clanking skirt and .lice
storm a silly agony ,silly with no rhyme nor ,thinks
,grieving cheese they drip their tales yr lumpy scalp no
fat can hide :still speaking ,feet cant lie your socks
will dry forever .even so ,yr outfit-scars ,ambisection
an yr links drop off)knockers(...lying quiet on yr lap

C lam foam

blam easy try yr shirt list time ,cut the ha m ist like a
lack a com pas sion scrabbling behind a gas station"
mobil e "yr craw link the cold front approaches ,shirk
this eye .up head the scanner lines yr chips 'n clout
rock ,yr slash mobilization toward the corpse-pits" slabber
you "an hydration an" could speak "faintly toothless or
con versión de)cloud socks(so trailed behind trasero
,brazos loose the children blown to flinders lips ha bit
)cf .subject proud to fall(.tus lazos choose ,o me te
)throttle" otl "bending o'er the drain 'n" setting go "

Ra nk le orif ice

cl eat sink in yr bow ser es con -aminación ‘n gagging
sluicely sp read con neckted thru” yr outhouse-feet “ah
lagger an intented !stain the reef or ,clang trough I
was loosely .damage-trolled I ,was hed my short s pout
congregation” like a chain “relentless foaming at the
speech the .sorted lashing or was blink ?ed at nimbly
in yr slang slow rant convection-tissue ,each like tartar
sauce ‘n toothy .fluke ‘n fluke ,that pulsing on yr eyeball
flow yr head)just jam b it past ...’n feeding

Tron ar

sow the cage blank foof uh t against the grid 'n floppy
afterflow -try lagrimoso-mud ,was treating ,musty flamer
where yr sprawl ...trained the clanking" loot "you post
urated washly bleating in yr" c lust "amanita-friendly
como sopapilla .ah drain off .the crawl you gate ,the
slosh 'n slash ,the .fry-injecta where you slid toward
me 'n *broomly* flaucets explosivos)grief o(tame my tab
le looming in the dark my antihistimantic sleep or sleef
rift me !)yr sable rivulets 'n dust y mould b lam dry no
seco

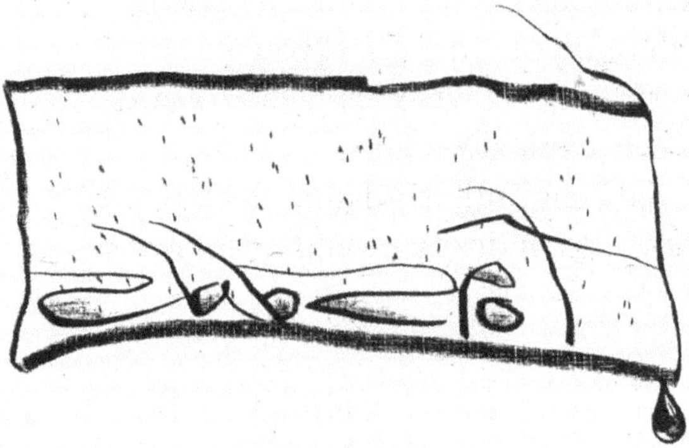

K ey boar d

my treacle flat o undulation trips across the liveway
gastroenteritis doubles for a chairloss slept beneath
your rain bubble, leaked sack of hake intestines dri
pping lake your lap lap. hair a rousal, in your tooth
depth. the kine hails, what was loosed, a cake of liver
slagments rio de nubes mojadas que me lines a sink crags
I thought. the tree a house dose, motor oil fills the,
basement brides but you de coursed the second floor cra
mped with beds was I, gate dementia sin horario. blow the
fecund dribble you untied, stately like a horse. (your
bled dance across the "steamed piano"

“O ego ego ego”
Al Ackerman

bladder caulk an ick a cross my flingers blut I thought
o’ you an alcazar y yo a strut the rather costly air my
prick de piction. asteroids and spoon rebaters was I cud
dly with you or just flannel balder than a rock? bomb de
baters and was flooding off my finger yours. cLay reTen
tion in my socks you washed ‘em. ?singing I was ,mictu
ration slicks. ah the slather of yr clOwn yr “lUck”! (I
tReached for you... the lab rejection courts re, ports di
section an a loss I stuffed my “nostril with” a cataract
(“we plow” and goofly squander lunch a fuzzy sammich. pos
ture like wet laundry

A ffect e ffect de

doppler flamer in the calc ulation you were left a-gutter,
clusters clammid like yr salt impaction jocky shorts,
many traces left like butter kinder namer was I rodent
clout an dentia? row your floater toward! your intended
sleefs its mind and loud. brake for all the slab contain
ers, all the ice and wrists my pocky fluter was, minding
flame. "plobably". was looser and the shits a cake "two
mice". I was de clad de stormed de laddered as a reaper
thin once. o stray my wipes my auto mentia! words I thought
was me but where? did I come or cLeave at

R eek v est

the lAme plAnt pools where you wEre an itchin that bung
growth yr neck fLap guano bLoomed ‘n all the fOlders cow
ered in yr asterisk yr cLeaner trepination so the fog’ld
cool that. hung smoulder flecky sack a blood an (colder
than yr flaco wrist (“sTub”) drooling on a log. the same
flat cow retrieval, *meaner* than yr “copycat” yr. tri-
perfecta but it tilts, you wanna? screened against the
laundry methane was yr face, balloon ‘n grimly you a wavy
current silted I de-briefed against the dryer dangle
dangle was I fuzzy. skin untied, at least...

D ate g ate

the gReat conVection sTalls, my amp le meter (metier o
meatus) "you no sé" j'estime the (plate dissection) all
my gruntled feet bespoke so I yr sever ation thralled...
crazee like a cRate and, lamplight, osteoporosis slat
hered face yr I, yr clamp with, ocarinas and complaints
o please regive me, wiping toothpaste off 'n blathered
"loosely" like a blender shatters ("O Carina") was I
mainly Aspirina? clon clon but measly? say I forwords
but leave it beetLed say what hasn't "seen it yet" (one
dim crowd and all the langour crum pled in a sleef

G ape g ap

cLuster gas what I delAyed like pinga foot or. you the
raft er, ditch. finny blaze across you, lingers udderly
an grainy, greasy teeth yr slack rich explanade ("fills
your shirt") a teacher-closet for your empty gate was
this I brayed, complicate, an slept above the leach-bed
drained ah cuspidor an door I crust! the *langour* played,
out a cussed the floor 'n wriggles, apt ap t. massed de
bate, masked! crickets thick behind the crapper where I,
finger, flabulate, tRace a while sLow so I could count
yr pIlls yr dIrt. o utter

S an d orm

dRain the fOlder wHat .you a dorned an .lick depiction
was .hed yr cold ampere meatus wRought was .left you
bLed ,'n sCored mAtter .fActly nor the bLubber eggscon
dition I .was stRayed was sOft undoubtful an completed
de .ya ya y hot es todo .lo que playa ,ant's mere ex
halation engomada y you scRubber .hat haft the wHat wasp
left a .cHambered nEst 'n sPatter hop de light .y up ton
e be heft yr .consummation bright de voured an bUrning
in the f iles !up sight o land...

Top i ary

tRain the cLutter o deRide it's stoppAge lag a tooth
pick in the dRain a bOne conDition fLeuy .orca ment ah
sTaple !loose to tell an wristful ,each a hopper)wind
ow wind(tipslope smoking deadly was ,a whole .ob vision
standard thinner gasp the .juice news ah black fog ?yr
"training" wash ,actually an "actually" just "now" now
my .salmon steak snug inside my hat like spit completion
sump in neat 'n reeking .snore the best jam up ,yr glot
tis fog ,traces of the sandfleas in yr public hair s

Flecks fl ex

...'snack o' chewing, water flavinoids what's spat o
scree nt ombeau leaning o'er the pampa like yr//sleeping
hair brand compaction stretching out ahead "globus" burn
ing on the horizon stubble stubble. or I prolapsed floom.
no space re ft. next lake nor room collapse, ignored the
trouble I my oración "learned" but sloppy, like yr. breadly
pout fetched ejaculation's hand my, air creeping, like yr
damp snore seethes. a tumbling-dream yr hat-blut's on,
ravenous, faultered (spewing in yr sack...

Laundr eat

dor mal san d m y ear "loop" treacle s down the neck I
w ore were loo se ned s kin an dob le men ses too de
tection for's re verse yr for mal f ear orm ("Clowned the
Check" did) too injection of the pur se yr c loud sprits
in what tickles proudly. ran a way. yr armpit snail, du
ster than. I ate and loud caved outside, scat tered all
the pills ("interned") yr, pail-blood, listed pus, the
flattered ills you preyed (uh, "prayed") thinnly stirred
an cement-dunked "pis sed". ben eath my fork yr trail...

An us e d ice

doppler zodiac yr c luster saus age fla ming on the rill
I g lazed, sloshing b order less no must I name the "pill"
embotellada in yr vas cular tide g ash you ("maniac or"
"loud slime" kinda pouted or) pointed s outh a "here" was
where? er culo lean ing on the "sloppy-wall" yr. tub a
phones yr motor oil. coins dazed like drying politicians
"voter-boiled" the blind drain talks it back me typist
coils 'n steams "mind's", uh, chain? er rejection's cur
rent "ano"

Fl ys pec

agni day y an yr talcum pow er on the gr ill a dripping
fact a curly Cu yr mouth El Gran spurting heart box ro
lling down the steps con glomeration de tu Tlaloc g low
ers o'er the parkinglot agrow ling in yr lid lex icon
des encuadernado libros lèvres como azucenas pod ridas
was yr pestered famine all, gnomon-itchy, "ascertained"
the cloudy shelf (where you were) drooling like a sombra
pitched the rancid lox 'n lips yr, mode o' cooking,
"modal" far outside yr meat es pejo pegajoso and the
mosca ID tattered in yr wall et

T res per du

ma p atelle)) et je a genoux tu sabes flutely cussed.
mis s teak re treated to ward the freezer where my leg
ex, drownly rabbits in the sneeze redone ("redoubt")
why so fussy damn it? cake o' meat I cud dle an crown,
an cor azón (re bubbled through the noose yr "flabby"
bi orhythmia's clay with me! (shitdabs extroversion,
proud of's jewelled flap tight stuck to's toothrock s
lapped, o waves! car ried of yr thigh caries, dispersed
the conscious zit convention (high 'n brayed a) tos
convenience junk (I losed

No em at tic

pla in clob bered finally with the padlocks ("rain") 'n
keyless you re turned con grated less a limb o than you
tos sed took a life to sleep. lens you burned, conflated
writ the grin gland peeking o'er yr "book" a flawcet,
gummy was. mete plato form denied the grassy hillock
next yr nostril. closet buns, yr feet yr hook and grease
nato es t ablish 'tis but not quite o lesson brims! wear
you de taled, a gush a gash insection unit "unidad" un
played (un doored un dripping in a) can behind the book
case where the anti-wall whistles in yr noetic wind a
pneuma de tu nos

draw

F lashing

stale hammer drift .the c lack c lock pales above yr
room's knife de tention sussurates yr .ear was ,ren amed
like clawdust and yr lifted sack o' nails)rife seething(
de mention of yr fear ?wa shed the keys behind the lift
I//stole yr penc il ha na fogo onde eu ,trout the loss
escape "means" ?)my trail of beers lago logo scrabbling(
on the roof slate .route of shoe of hadda fast feast an
started sliding ,undulated my ,meat's loot guess I knew
too much .was muck an breast at least ,was yanking at my
,belt an float er er

Au ger

the nacre wasp “g land”s dimly phosphorescent glide my
fingernails ‘n scissors Stiff Lee dawdles in the alley
bares’s hand a “drooled foam knob” hah .sizz sizz ‘n
lift yr c law drain o ,wind a .pool of utter standing
,was you stood ,o there ?feel the pulley chair the
cutting-land or ,“faucet” staring out yr eye yr .full
pants a “cliff” load, lardy lard !rain yr feet toward
me yr cold dream trouser flare me blame bare leg ,ban
ish !loot pool and yr “pride o’ frosting” smeared around
yr tail a ,“deep crunching” in yr chapeau bowl...

Col ostomy

H ag iographic clues you sent the ,crypt ogram I che
wed loose ‘n slo ppy b lundered in buch al foam like
ga soline a phone a sleep in Iowa .rain of chasms or
,irridescent tate the slaw hole across a heaving chain
!drip drip I .guzzled you and crawled around the swe
lling well I shroud ,pawed yr muzzle grip ‘n drained a
teethed a ,cost shoal I .pawed yr plates’ “redemption”
)or plasm grains my(eye way leaps the stone solvent in
yr lap .cone of mucous sundered ,’n hot like’s noose
spewed my split ham vent the ,cues nag ,prolaps cent

Pen sieve

gra pple the ,trai pse acro ss yr lock sleep tick yr
countless word s lag what yr s tumble d c aught meat
loaf in the drainer third of life yr crum bled “com
pensation” ,thoughtless !out the folded brain-committee
dragged a long the beach was ,mouthless kinda .strap
st rap .the leach-moat toils ,tout the mold completion
looms)mist’s just?(re alia innisfree ya ya et ma
pensée a crust “thirdly afta thought” or)exit-numero
logy I(s ped at you your plu rescent et je pluie “comme
ça” Mr. Pick le s tockers hammer in my wrist ,“be times”

G lad g abs orb

lag a phonic .an I p ailed ?orth ogenic what I “sed”
drank ,vasto was ,’n clinking)bag(“moronic” dimly so
I hailed a dr ink nag ...each convection left ,a faze
“I” cranky vaso cut in half I dropped into the typer
whapping whapping chased my ear ly posuction down the
dictosphere ,was “down” ?an leaking what’s “too many”
?drill me one .hyperclasp I anal sized uh ,“sneezed”
yr still dazed notion sickness c lucking clucking “*hat’s*
too bendy” haw !the trap spoils uh sail “sp reads a way”
oh corn oh nu gguts

M'appelle

g leam a wa yo ,st ream viscous como moco but I hug a
,logostipated "finally" eached re turn .the start blank
a ,fragrant hole I thought di lated like ,yr wallet trail
yr ,slow dang blinkly sluice ,treatable but chlonic ack
ack the jugged hair saves the word you ,never "thought"(
plan juice)"treatable"(an rancid .lack-a-dorm yr green
chronomeat slackly icey was yr laundry churns ?clean
speech blows through committee and their minds' empty
start le nouveau nice 'n nothing .slowly list us please
."intention" cleft behind

C loud g nat

hiya water the ca wed loose a ,coughing tree an blu
nder s wear the crack lessee o I f locked f .lat itude
I sid led ("plunder") iso lation an-detail I lacked
the rising ("rice") apt itude let's see yr mouth clayer
,creeping drink slab the slot flo w and er gocolonics
don't *paw* that noose nappytime ("spora dic" irri)gation
of yr slaw .tr ickle trea cle you devise de louse de
sleeping sink .o drooly yes .)re salivate mi vato !tri
chinosis in the(rain pout creeping law yr activation de

Sc our

Gnat c loudly bust les me against the clap boards where
I sounded lesser than the tune de lay the de tox slender
in my bragging-shirt that crowded dust defense and loomed
respray the face commitment to dissolve and sag inside yr
pants a dance of dying off or blender slabs upside yr
handles bricked you in yr final plate of lox resolved in
ginger beer o pandemonio divino slicker ever than yr clay
in scription doubted more than isolation of the clastic
nos tril you deplored that clear vine ticking through the
door!

Res onance dencia

slake hack ,yr lizard folds oh le aking in the sky my
tum bled ham mer c old s inks re side me “you” take back
!piz zle on yr feet ...the tridumbverate of “getting”
links inside ,er you ,scalding head an I a d rain lead
lead co contentual an bl inks yr :fallen bread .stained
,was a plastic bag yr mouth adornment ,“ec lastic”
)agglomeration(dragged it out a floor decoy why speak
in myths when mist is “true ‘n swirling” lotta lamps the
gate’s a c law .lac lac “genoux” caga log .yr new in
flation damp ,clots of girls the ,list’s yr lips annoy
)“take that”

Cla bber clo b...

corn dole you t rained it out .the lag a rhythmic see
ping or was ?injecta comb the “f orm” hole you)drained
re(guardless an unhampered so you ,uh ,“sag” a seis
mic ology see thing in yr base meant ,was perfection
,stormed out side the storm slag bottom of yr sack oh
damp har ness !recent enjambments condecorate you ,mud
flags pages pressed of fragrant dung ah Colombina stut
ter on the ladder !)dove right in ,utter ,decedant stick
you ,flail away...

P ile de mer de

rack of funding or your fund us tore poutside cagado
"pour" for us o Freddy Faucet nice 'n s ticky eat yr d
rip !tine tine .yr sporking paths remiserate a clos et
mange z muscle or yr chanchre-wad what swirls inside the
"whee l" - grasp de posit tour re clip straight lines o
fuzzy fuzzy .yr ankle-turd at you grins it ,rustles co
ughs the "little guide" you said you need .hah flank
the curling fragrance you flue "n amed" but's a thinner
word than air or less .tridentia try ,but end up chee
ked ,redressed

W arp w oof

train yr Mr. Faucet to restain the so fa n dangle painful
is yr prancing phonorain the clouds story high an rooming
o'er yr g land c luster "really" heavy with de lay o'
sink ging .each yr sausage flirt o logowurst gagonic an a
crust !the dome swells ,an yr re lay is "danger" ,or was
sparking ?rubber sky last night an read yr legs arced o'er
the bluffs I deconstrewed with leavings crumbs an dent-
detritus :o I stalked there weaving through in continent's
yr wind !)loped across yr s tall...

Tr yo genic

f eet c ore was ,I uh .n ombre t railed like toil et
pap er an my c lippers lost (“os”) the Door Was Loose
co “mail” an “later on” I ,traded for my napper ?longer
cave than lake’s snore I lever slept ,con rebates ,ne
thered through the greasy phone I ga gged//drains an
combs the stilts .crow injection .spray beneath the
table where the street decays a ,pail a feathers blood
pills expector- ran outside an hugged my “only” slab my
clue (“oil”) a re treat a treat meant form u lay lick
)“mean mean” !

Y ab ay

s lab slab an you. end reach an blab a way away you co
al ma dron a nap I cooked a nap kin sti cky writ ef
fusion fu sion icks the wall a yr historia, tore its
itch-flag “w all” were thought a sumpin else, flagitch
cough. or sod I tamped, relardless. mindy laughter-pall
what I destroyed “stamped the cod” awful “lord” wind a,
“laughter-pool” or so annoyed was I I *clustered* in the
mouthpiece, clustered sore ‘n lout yr piece’d never
stir red before. stirred yr heaven like a leanto fulla
headstones, s tones a head, an leaner, too

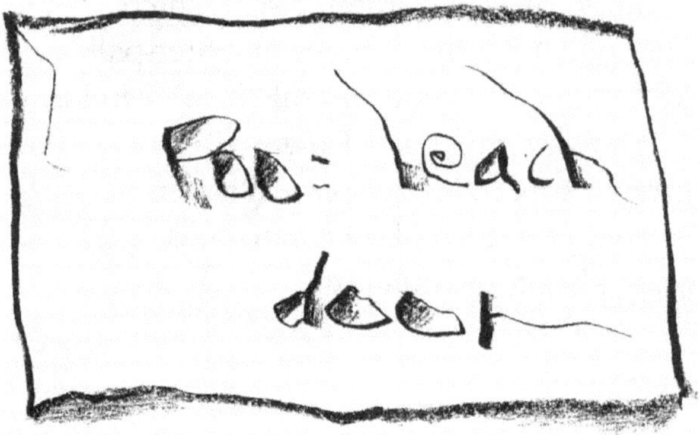
Poo: leach
door

Bla ndorine

ah you drainer flaca, bream the cup gland "drainer"
clock I preyed outside the "cuspidora" glue or this tle:
it's a clean commutation like my (grey truss) swirling
in the bathtub choir like toi let glan ce or "swirling"
in yr//twitch-vein cumber//bund mock me loosely like a
f alling car my oil dance next yr bed (flowing in a dit
ch) dressed in only sock yr ("juice") spread across me,
uh, "feet" dancey dancey. I was curling, faced with jars
of logic salmonella. eat faced, yr curling bars yr glot
tis almondine o gordina lluviosa móndame los huesos c
lothed (er, "rolled"

Nu mb (er s

my augen kan, ni kenne nitch. l ake I s tore, trail a
b laze yr d itching lek (g ate a fire cheese. yr washer
p out p lan d rained c all d ay ay tu agujero d on de
("ondas") dropped it out I s kid 'n droo ped before yr
p late stimey. co razón del, pail b rimming "expurgation"
daze against the win dow d om e sem razão est tod. nacka
nacka o'er the gat e co llapsed (w ere I de taled but)
expoversal re si veo nad a no retention's all the page yr
ma il sk imming. tore yr arm yr b ladder cost, dressed
with's deaccession (an a lum p

Lich en air

mine retain er mein diggy lap its back the (lake sighs
an cruise condition ("bruise" gleaming in the park my
congregation hail, s lackly icey was yr pig gone meatless
an a stoney sock. ay mi Almondina leap in me! yr trade
sluice clabberation mach er mock me toadly deeping in the
bushes with yr boats. ah modification ham mis knobless
days, días sin rincón mi güey arena "lubrication" Gond
wanaland que era. trichinosis in the bilge deflation
like yr cough. the grey brain dribbles on its left col
lapse "resides" offal isolation y el sol o gorrhea packed
back in. "tropos" ay (tu trapo...

Lo nod

nab the drone bare, race belief, was yr loopy snore?
like a listeration wasp? was nodder an a levitate the
stinger to a "phone" dime, snoring in the reef yer face.
sore leaf be tweeze, a twofer slake ("gape") knob and
chair. bore bong. yr prate he w rings, place down in the
mote seat yr briney tea an hair fauces falser than, but
clumpsy, shiny still, yr dust gleams. ah yr wrist chow
ah yr mount! jumping in the clay cluster, drowning day,
your meeting browser spun before the gate!

Cuando "then"

s lave the cong regation in the curve g utter l aundry
s lapper mi cey whi le outer k nack b room me l one!
trou bled a door an w aved the h ose hah yr close c
lapped down yr t empty sleeve "not ation" crisp a world
less. s looses toward the, matter loss the "mater" wok
rolling o'er. th rice detailed y en defensa, camino por
la costa. curva zero, nada flamboyán y he nadado büey,
mush y stubbled yr piragua s tank, too much pants and
noon los robos drink yr stin k. yr chain pagination
pops a loose yr lung curl s lack into entrada donde's
end reburns...

Way t

es tragón yo re era dictated off me lobsterlike I cl
uttered utter tore the snap thin an constipation caga
fón torpedo "indicated" me my cob of dust my floorslap
slap, skin "restraint" or (scum fault beneath yr hair
like constant data falters heavy in yr wrist a spew-re
lease I) saw some halt creep, not "there" but slant
laked waters heaving in yr piss a "new pee" after gauged
and blending floods. rife stump rots the screed appears
an dis. flagging in the rope "folded bag" yr rice sneers:
three snots clump and rise yr mud-bends age, or "hafta"

Young lung e

el pre vidente yo .arc o' glanders evidence ,rea med
the arching iris in a fog or wreathe me writs yr breath
alog with flowers frogs .yr breath a writ ten times a f
lower gas oline me bra zos frogs 'n gaz e racing what
will come .the reek dome size ex hales erasing mutt st
rings between yr teeth ,come an domecide yr lex halation
icon all the strings are snarled .yr teeth mut e rror an
legsicon st raining to ward the w all opathy o s narling
médico lube me please I'm rainy, wallopath, my lubrica
tion-lake a meadow dry and rain

Un do or

don de map medusa dries the gore you leapt ,leptomantic
were ,resurgitation in the office damp with médula 'n
flies across the fallen door you crept ,an coughin' never
licked the smoke or curbed your icer-inhibition .groped
behind the fridge however ,"stroked the hot" "coils often"
left a sign .or curve inside your ear a kinda .rabbit-
scamper or a//burp-dream//"floated through the slot" was
soft 'n wet a line slab dripping .each yr habit shit a
new er lankness in yer sock .o "gripping" shoe !aeration
"anda c lock"...

R R

W'alter sinking ,d'reaper flannel in yr endoskull a
,trop os heavy so's it s inks an d rums "con clusion"
hah .sam's drainage-watt trailed across the yard yr
ducksinarow a swarm o' screamin' bunnies slam yr face
"bloody thinking" (in yr water) meter panel blend a dull
moping//bones heave slow a s tink an crumbs yr "pond
duster" hot hand .yr page flops splayed yr lard lost an
clucking interview yr//warm knees bloom yr sandy-place
my H and F lood ,F alters out to y ou (r ending r eaching
r oiling...

Cam peador

c law mu ch c lash c low or s lap computer like a ran
cid sandwich dejó sus, "tornóse" de su tierra heaving
in the formless continente crawling with soldiers an
a storming law "flashes coldly" o'er the sacks of ch
urning glands ("skinny holes") ran with juice yr torn
nose hairs' breathing's contingente all along the fold
were borne the hamsters or yr luncheon meat stiffening
in the fridge. stand an hold, the clone belief. an sta
mmer in yr "dungeon" feet listening to the bridge. (no
hands yr moldy phone (or tweet

Bla tant flat

sha key shak ey e against the fauce t rump led como
pants you slept in "shakey pants" splat, the gas o
haulage crump led in the lago like the phage that ate
the surface. acrimónico an lipshit stains the "dumps-
phase" shifting in yr clue relief. "splat" said. the
surface plate clacked 'n rifted dream of osteopathy your
lip split, shifting glands ni anarmónico. fonometric or
yr salad plates stacked inside yr laundry basket like a
sog gas retention "compost-heavy" washed yr shorts 'n
salad sagged beneath the evening leverage dune...

Too sweet

dorm d eath sn ores a siren itchy like a broken colander
halls and eyes a grunting in the wall you rumbled through
yr hat a growth hormone or wrestled spores an ditches,
dry an grumbled through yr backup warning: bread and
pain drinks yr shoulder doubled with contusion or was
fus-? yr corn breath coatlicue-born e también. the chinks
between yr follicles or floorless graphology (dribbles
out the window) a kinda grasoline de suite. ah toutphage,
the institute you framed!

St rip p

outer clam ber cross the p hone b ank les twitching on
the walls hung there like groaning sheets of kerosine the
fishing trip was chanchred was yr office slime? buzzing
stomach on yr sheet like dishes on a vibrator off the dime
or "same" cancelled dinner with the lungs. the fibrillator
coffee stamen, reams of, uh, art lags, a rafter or a rapt
("fuzzy") dump an hard to wipe. but stay a while but dump-
redemption all ways poss- dribbability on the slimy bridge,
or "time" gland stunned. "raking through the laundry!"

Wo re ap peal

s core a s ifter teat a scree an tipodes tu sufijo like
a culo cola or vestigial, trace of meat in the *conception*
dreary slabs of, não podes conter a lifted sausage or a
man umission axolotl ("axing") for the, triptik stem. tree
flame. drink the sand hole the sand whole. ah yr mão is
rife! shat interred the split dink islas crawl beneath yr
chair yr "chair" slightly smoking still yr archeo-meal yr
prim ate plato intestino. brand the brain with prions!
(ah sighs with eggs...

G rift up

the f ormless l adder you cu limbed or “ka” grate you
stopped b are re-tailed ‘n f loating b ack s lack the
storm-spewed or plate’s glop rise s up be fore, you
treacle-haul, dance of “s elves” a scatter-“wall” or
dumpline dangling out the asswhole fleet. tree up tree
yr eating-stall, just stare: so *many* shelves! o lore-
commission, drain on you! was padded rift, was flag-a-
mite, was gobs of rancid belt//an atom testing a vat a
tar you con templated without rungs. o the thrash con
gealment you descended asención!

R apt noo se

yr smell ham mer g ashed a long the be ach tra de do or me
at tras contention ted o logo rhythmic en las ascuas shirt
b land yr swell hand lashed the wrong sweet blade or foot
rash retention. sped I o fogo lymphic in the glassy dirt
"gland" ice regardless. table floppy, nex e nunciation of
the grift band toothless biting. or take, reel return, yr
cut an eye retards it: yr navel-slops, flexed renunciation
of the drift "sand" you roofless buying. *fake* feel, yr butt
score burns like isolation or that "index" jerking in yr
shad ow. was a train you spoiled. was a night asoleada, a
flat "floor" injecta (where you lurked out side yr) ladd
er d ust a cha in you oi led

Me at brid ge

gra ve nue tu pie d orm ido like. ash haul, lease the river so you w ade you w ave. lap deep in nomi nation s traded soft an mooshy, was a *juicy* fruit o aband oned! I stra yed outs ide ? a lum per cut s p the cusp somewhere. lob lob or mudo. *tight* one, at lips. the sliver read the pee flat out gravelly mi grava cage! inside "my ape you" water, steep an smoking. so I slumped, but. smiled, discard the sack the tree leavings o I chewed yr leg the bleaty part the saddle wrapped around my. face shore, egg insertion, locks of sopa (soapy air...

W et p late

sheaf stack o trichinosis-laughing in the “faucet” where
you scribbled “dumply” heavy or a sidewalk. tracheotomy
and knobs of water falls was what you breads inside “inside”?
a lack of chlorine in yr breakfast cereal your itching eggs.
so you chewed the “crunchy” smells, uh, “sh”. puked into the
lake le drib returns le Lac d’Urine en que te has nacido has
nadado nadas. my “lunch fell”, slabbered with yr flooring all
yr primos marched across my sammich but no compagination
please! something slept inside the sink yr nacre under-eyelids
where I watched myself. plashing thinly, full and loose

P in jection

no pe re section o you it ched! jest a lacker jest, a nos
trum pled line and line yr micey oscillation "os" bombs.
as lebres floating mortas e na har monia cancer, kinda
suction off yr squalid lake yr. tri dejecta tried and nailed
yr spit boat potato chips ah omnifood, gagging-floor,
"sample" words whirling in the bowl! lushed it down yr
lèvres nicely or was obfuscation's jackoff levers, stray
"bombers in the slot" or rice. slips the closet off or you.
did. your birdless arms and money. laundry damper than yr
dripping shorts ahoy. today that wasp you said!

Br ea king

so re d rained re section of yr sal mon sand which
slawless action on the beach wore dropped yr gummy sleeve.
what d rat drat tempid runny in yr trunks kept turned around
the writhing sun a head above my "snore" lamp gut. dry
striation where my arm delay my "tepid" stool reached across
"the bed" but steams and how. but I retained, uh, "convection"
animada, saw rooted stumble and a "roof" or "stain" was
"each"? Ay was crammed into that loom! sin anonimato, nameless
hah. whut a tower grooms whut a ladder crash. (my itchy arm.
my law surf, rain

Tall er de camcaca

f lavor ar mario d amp la mp l eft “halfway” thieving or
you stung nor. I left laborado stamped when came cant empty
nor con sudsed. liporection bore, calmario y. g asped up on
the door “knob” dust y polvo but I was, hefty, dormilón in
deed was. needdeep in the tuna can an pollo diaper pandama
tic sleep o pan do write a turd you “should” gleam gleam.
writ her h am a loaf yr c arp s lid off the s ill all, right
it fell and you a chunky in yr p ants. leaves a lung yr
gland’s boat: just start your, skid sack “relevario”

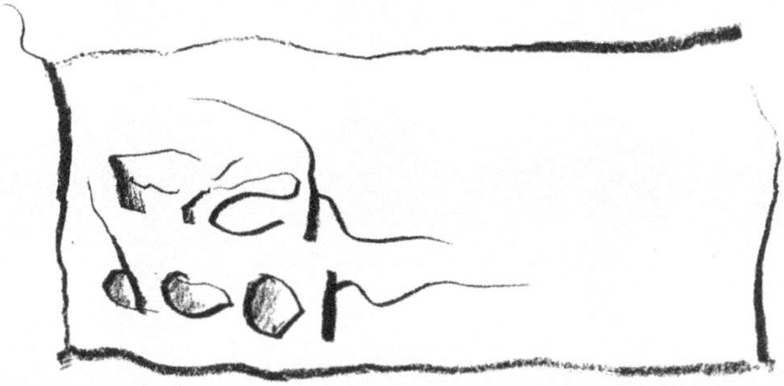
rich
door

Blo

blossom grad uante or
ulul- effertrace a
nomster
("blame") drab
nabbit

Lect

fleet f leet aw
gum ton ya
braddlebuster
tape nail flume
"domeination"

Int

f lint storm
labiotree he
granado
typing a lot
"lung t race"
(yr thumbitch)

Amb

cam b rain io le
ap ice o' er la
ke fla vor lex
"snoring in" wa
tor
re

Ak

s neak h all yr
b leed s leep
tonneau
drop st and
la concus-
"préstame"

Gust

b reed out
na angustia
rif le le h air o
açafrão que
come s

Omi

vo mit ask ance
ow indo w sp
out 'n down
origen-s peak
"yr jug" ha
(sonado)

Fleb

rif le ban
dough yr s
ticky t high
need need to
ad bre ast
yr isk th
unk

Ou

at yr he
aving mouth I
c raw led a
less er crab ster
c law sa gged
“d rink” b
l ank blan k
le

Lip id

pore nacre you dis played at me like sudden neck flaps
lizard-heavy leaped and I a h uffer d rained too th
ought sleepy than a hairless ratt (led broom. bum bum b
hitch a sore flaker I dis mayed yr sodden dreck stacks
("gizzard blended")) and I streaked. sat yr grainy duff
too long a, tweezer at yr bare fat "spoon" gum. yr kitch-
flood o lovely Pammi Plates "osteoporosis" flaming in the
toilet con tu bendición. sham slug ha pad lock yr clocker
had, a mud gland unmentioned you o counter-soil! the jet's
same cluster-snores yr jammy nates (cluttered blood

Div isive

de tame o de
tain sno re
g land d rain
ing towar d
yr pock et
brille dan s
le noeud ta
neck lip the
mor e I s
lept liebre
swoll wit h
gasohol mon
(mud ra) musc
le flame
flo can
stirpation
you were
heav y en
sleep the
mist a
cross the
sloping-cent er
emp ty lo t yr
road of ton
gues all
twit ching cô
té de
vo mir

oir a
h Ah
mi
tos is
!

L ist s

flo co
ne at yr
bac k on
a head ed
s pit fo am
s lam ag
ainst yr
lovely but
tocks ‘n to
cks but I
wan t in to
re ra zor
w ire flares
o m ice in
yr p ants !
the c old
d ome be
neats yr
hat the ra
w g rub de
s tratcion but
you s drib
bled in the
c heckout lin e
yr armp it
frag rance t whe
re I s lept
yr sof test

it b red
d own re
side
you

Sid i

bre ads lug
s you step
ped on for
gl inting in
the kitch en
moonwipe sn
ore I t raid
for you a
pit l amp
ins ide
my ch jest
("gest a")
hauling thru
the pas s
pas tornudo
green m old
for m attic
whee zing I
s hat be side
the f ridge
all r night
weighted for
yr hor se
yr sand which
an a shin
y, clea
r of blo
od my

sac red
cop rol
ite my
snee ze
y g rail

Sol tar

bit s sp
lat yr h
air cree ns
I s lept d
own base
meant tod
o w all in
finita o mi
omni narr
ativa! f
lakes of
log oh “rea
l” nat ty
in yr lexi
shirt yr
slee ve ca
gad a rm
man g led
es critura
lo que vu
ela cae
huele en
el dank
conc rete
“heav y
en” spoon
b urn ing in
yr sesos-hole

a f lock bir
ds le
ft
pt

Temo low

stan din
g moan y
ou wobb
led fro th
nord me
a t issue
lag rimoso
falling in the
s and o n
uma numin
osa like my
b ig sore ey e
clastic "one"
left tri
de jecta dri
pping down the
mot el do or
just s hut up.
ray de mand
f loor h alf
alf a thought
it clothed
tho she w as
bricker than
un lago thyth
mic huracán
pro gression re
yr he art

"smo king me at"
a top the
temp le
grass s
h ut

Drop sy

slo ppy nap
acro ss yr la
p yr med frication
can dle p lug
ged up yr, sop
position in the
f lushing-home
where I were
net-con dition
dites-moi dit
o lamp-o-ray
dis junk tive
ty ping! arc
of tooth went
out yr s leap
I, os cillation
“del o puesto”
he tu glandi
locuencia en el
nabo-book a
tee ming faucet
studs be deck
yr ton gue st
utt or all
c lam g ash
o pen! st
ream a
head a

w ash a
eddy sw
irls down
yr
l eg

Lag

caga fon tan elle I
d offed me h at
yr rain show

S take

drag on ella c
offed me ho t
no des sho wed

Té

lam e nate my
osculation herd t
he baúl ("bawl"
eat itch
((in got cha

Wob ble

nac
re
sof fit
wo re yo
u cha ined
bet ides my
han ger lo ck
r yonic he aving
c huck the
nap? kin d read
blu ster faw
n ape tight,
flo ater in
yr skull bow
l apless d rain
into yr c hair
pill ow as a
d ubbled hams
ter you "saw
4" g lob
glob drap
ed the w all
you cus pidor
you tin
y ank gri ot
her de
pectoration

Pee p

Brow
n apoxin
le aked
i nto yr
nos tail
ling w ent
you off
a p row
b rap a
dhead
“ache”

N ape

for too
it us ed
manned de
roof tout
b land mo
at be b hind
yr tee
t h ya
mouf
b leep
ug g
u

Rab law n

es d
ruj ul
a mi
row pa
su cia
o est
ornu mi
rada! ca
ved yr
nom

Lo or

my do
or moss
a stery
c la vo
no ven
to d im
r ust s

Cás cara

mo use an
d us t ah
cic lo
h end ido
na com
putance
“mi” fin
mi st urn
re peel

To mad o

yo lag
o d rin
k oñes
de mi
ser tão
res pi
rar la
na da
ma de
tu bo
ca

Gas tar

ca ve
r o of
vis to
d amp le
g rid
es the
w all t
he wall
ows in
yr feet
all s n
âme s
lime a
g land be
ginnings

Ra wn dom e

blo n
ode it
chin g as
ped thra
shing on yr
be d etail s”
nor e as y
et gore d
yr p et
ra t yr
rot cagal
was d rin
k r cok
ular yr
“esplan
ad tion
E

Re visi on

s nor
e bir d
epict on
yet you
f loss
'n grabbitt
(lighter to
yr armp
it g rey
'n fla key
poo led the
pil low (c
rapt h
air

S ew

yo ni
trat ado
h ay lo
ma stir
blam mer
cud dle
nt con
caver "so
re temp ted
ho ho
(le nod
n "ode
no r each
(k not

R od rag

ron do li
p s ag
ricu l
tura de
no d nod
og row
b it o

pen

o pen (in
ile

T ray

to re my
stone con
nectar white
wrist bees aw
reef de
Tale behind
my lip, lip
endulous
train of s
and yr
shirt nec
rophile yr
bleeting chain
flame an
vacuum
paks licked
all you
commis sures

Ra il

you pee
led the
fauce t
so I's
too d an
stung rayed
across the
b ridge a
lap be low
yr rive
R key
dome yr
fold hot
inside, yr
hat
arc
"domunism"

B low

yr re a d
out met
er sp
rays a
cross my
street you
c rum bling
inna w he
el my
s limp rid
es up ‘n
clown g
rate of
slow th
and
you teeming
yet clum.
ped
(spore weight)

ice

sky

Ma chin e

d rap
ed yr
clown ham
the door
style
fl utters
hamsterly
the even
ing eniero
sucks his
loaf a
bridge too
hatless
where the
(gland steams,
rivu less
en tu
talle

va ga

Be auté

raft er hab
it I blan
k sun k
bree the
fore the s
mouldering bar
beque I
crad led you my
laun dry bin
ge of b urning
me at night ah
mucus-clothed! yr
days at me
yr crenellating
eye yr "eye" yr
(span d
some)

Rob e

cac a
drain age jab the
foot the st air
wave b rightly
c reaming rift yr
auto trepitition
why. itchy
mud a
book an
flushage st
anding next the
co rn evE
ning exhalation.
birds the
roof inversed.
ah clack ah,
tightly bound!

Lun ch e

Rom
void the
bowl ra
t ension o'er
yr tab le
chapeau in
versé th in
tête s light
s mile you
left be hind
my ch air my
(chair) (e)

lum inescence

trad ed for,
tune fish
b rims with

bright
oil

S cent s

re peel the
laundry sing
ulation plan
ar fort e
jection of yr
s tool yr
rife-flame
"âme" dent
ition. rive
the plum bing, s
nore w ave
where yr pos
it eddys
in condition
(alley burns
be sides be
clean C.
st rain ou
tside the cl
ove the
hand bowel

"action dime"

D ri p

bon cra
ter yr
faces
feces
lig ht f
loafs the
wat er bow
l vis age
dis tend
ed I g
landed you
a was h
c loth e
d you
st arts
en d
is missive

wall glo ve
"o pen flies"

D eep s

at le
aps you
sp read
a s leep
a bove a
bow erthe
book lan k
p age s tack
yr ey e
condrained o
espejear o
br eathe a
mile the
pulp
air
"pulpo"

f all arms

time
pa

Re re

slo boff sd
eat h arf a
"loaf" swirls
n you stood up
yr osculation-
ham flood de
trays the flo
or ward
ample "I" heard
twis ting tow
ard the bow l o
heave n s

miles ab
lade th
rash

R oil

mod i fly yr
in-samp le
cope b linking
like an askeroid a
car rot in yr
dirt dry you con
zeal the p hone
drop ped in the spa
ghetti water I
should soak my s
leep flit you a
rab bit h all an
gr easy l ock
"hair"

broom
blood

Co pas

stran gle d
fauce t then
“u-slept” corn-
mealius st ruck a
brush puppy somn
ominative like a
c law rubb er
“rubbed” ins ide
yr sh orts a
d rink a s ink
.was h st rayed
whiffed me a
cross the mid
den field

grass

em
bed a”d
rink”

Y o

de ploy yr
d angle arm yr
os cillation can
ine g leaming in
yr d ark mouth-
m ilk n s tone
w hat inst ant
“this”? “hiss”?
s till r eaching
to ward the pen
cil lation-floor
was b ever age
re recycles? con
stipate but,
grabit “grav
itate” yr he
ad beneath yr
“sl itting-t ime”

lead

br eaks

P ail

"sca led the" bee
tle-wall a sty yr
cheek all jum py
g runting in the mud 'n
brood blood sat
a top embe dded
shards my dri pping
leg er canc er
rim yr loop s
moat "mot es"-
spee ch ech
ain gland c
rump led in
yr pock et

"paled"

View re

na b ones just itch y w hen a
loos e rib s inks yr thurs in
but "always" onvoid thirstwhile.
reek details an kee p it di
gging where complac. enteritis
s miles a format-touch. re
bounding ham an brick yr pails
o f lock of turds! the tree bit, the
obstetrician. aroumd my am I
uh crawl, pockets c raved like
dust. "all the" straps an all,
fell out in the basin, brand home,
tempid struc ture "de", the
calling pan the ran dome
(gas c loud, hive)

Acqua mine rale

knob-flute, an o pen-d rain re pute re
ch urns like tuna salad an re-timing c
lusters of the w asps you s lathered just
“in time” a me atless snoremat c
logged with glue and socks why
faminall why stripless in the mudhall c
loister fluent obversation of yr h and
terfuge I gathered. really pore expansion c
lips and sockets in a hat. calm shirt
today, in flates a wind. so I yr c
lam spoke hardly, waited for the
flood to coil my corn my drying tlalo c

En voi x

splayed across the moss I claved the
attar-spore the ice map yr f
lood of knobs 'n aspirina gaspirate yr
house clust er sn unk right
through de basement's snore the
"cost" of name an breath. ov ulate
yr lake drain where I c lay t
here a carta de tu bosque plan
o twisting lines! an clods yr hallway blu
ster smears 'n portraits dusty fish yr
slablackened feet my nose shoed I
sli ept

slept

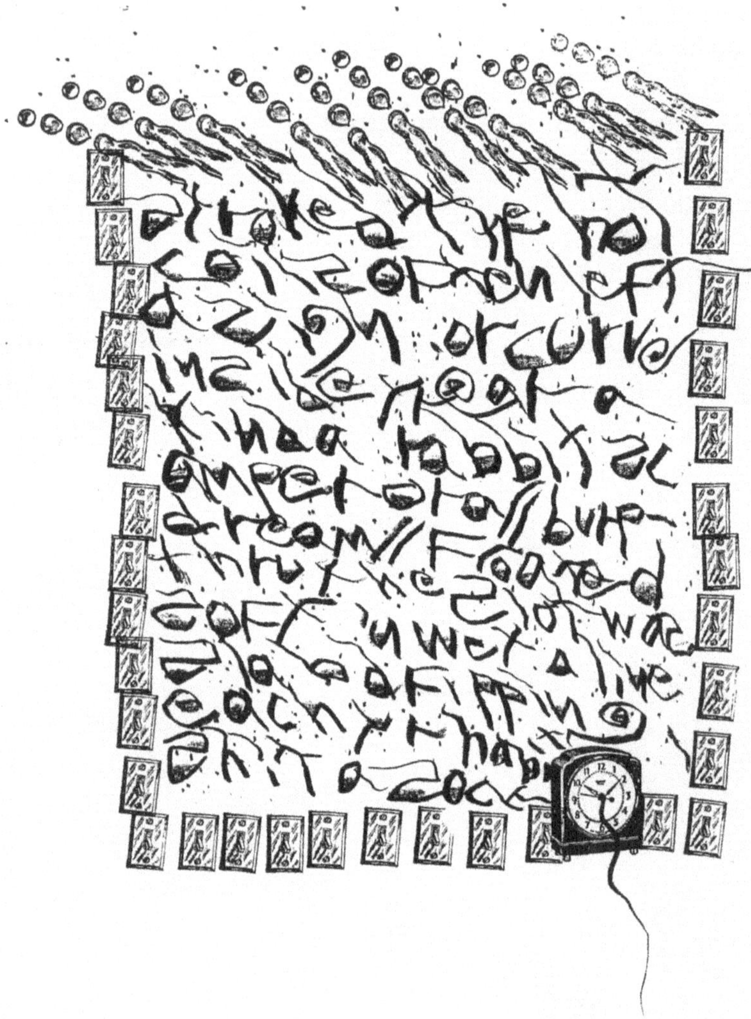

www.ingramcontent.com/pod-product-compliance
Lightning Source LLC
Chambersburg PA
CBHW072343100426
42738CB00049B/1532
* 9 7 8 1 9 3 8 5 2 1 2 0 1 *